I Give
You
Texas

500 JOKES OF
THE LONE STAR
STATE

I Give You Texas!

By BOYCE HOUSE

500 JOKES OF
THE LONE STAR STATE

Illustrated By
WINSTON CROSLIN

WILDSIDE PRESS

FIRST PRINTING SEPTEMBER, 1943
SECOND PRINTING OCTOBER, 1943
THIRD PRINTING OCTOBER, 1943
FOURTH PRINTING NOVEMBER, 1943
FIFTH PRINTING DECEMBER, 1943
SIXTH PRINTING DECEMBER, 1943
SEVENTH PRINTING JANUARY, 1944
EIGHTH PRINTING FEBRUARY, 1944
NINTH PRINTING APRIL, 1944
TENTH PRINTING JULY, 1944
ELEVENTH PRINTING OCTOBER, 1944
TWELFTH PRINTING NOVEMBER, 1944
THIRTEENTH PRINTING JANUARY, 1945
FOURTEENTH PRINTING JANUARY, 1945
FIFTEENTH PRINTING FEBRUARY, 1945
SIXTEENTH PRINTING MARCH, 1945

Other Books by the Same Author

TALL TALK FROM TEXAS
OIL BOOM
WERE YOU IN RANGER?
TEXAS RHYTHM (Poetry)

To
Poet, Historian, Folklorist
CARL SANDBURG

Table of Contents

TUNING

UP

Texas occupies all of the North American Continent except the small part set aside for Mexico, Canada and the rest of the United States.

"With Maine and Maryland upon her bosom,
    Rhode Island and Delaware upon her knee,
She can mix a Tom-and-Jerry
    For her sister, Tennessee."

The chief pursuit of Texans used to be Mexicans and Indians. This was back in the days when Texas was so wild that not even the law of gravitation was obeyed.

Texans are so proud of their state that they can't sleep at night. If you could open the head of a Texan, you would find a map of the Lone Star State photographed on his brain.

Texas owns the north bank of the Rio Grande, the only river in the world that is navigable to pedestrians.

In Texas, a man's social standing is measured by the dis-

1

tance from his front gate to his front door. On one ranch the distance is thirty miles—and the owner is thinking about moving his house further back as he is disturbed by the noise of passing automobiles.

Texas is so huge that, if you used the northern line of the Panhandle for a hinge, you'd put Brownsville so close to the Arctic Circle that the Mexican hot tamale peddlers could exchange their wares with the Eskimos for polar bear steaks.

Texas is bounded on the north by the Northern Lights, on the south by the invisible lines of equinox, on the east by primeval chaos and on the west by the Judgment Day.

If all the mules in Texas could be made into one mule, he could kick the "man" out of the moon. If all the bales of cotton grown in Texas could be made into one stack, you would have a stairway reaching to the pearly gates. If all the hogs in Texas could be made into one hog, he could dig the Panama Canal at a single root of his mighty snoot.

And if all the steers in Texas could be made into one steer, he could stand with his front feet in the Gulf of Mexico, one hind leg in Lake Michigan, the other in Hudson's Bay—with his tail—brush the Aurora Borealis out of the Alaskan skies.

And that's no bull!

* * * * * * *

A Texan was talking in the smoking car of a train in the East. None of his listeners had ever visited Texas and he wanted to impress them with its greatness, so he said:

"You can enter Texas in the morning, travel all day, go to sleep and then when you crawl out of your berth next morning, you will still be in Texas."

The others didn't seem much impressed, so he decided to stretch things a bit:

"And you can travel all that day, too, and you will still be in Texas."

One of the listeners leaned forward and said:

"We've got trains like that in Arkansas, too."

TAKING OFF

A Texan remonstrated with his son:

"I heard you asking a man just now what state he was from. If a man is from Texas, he'll tell you; if he's not, there's no use embarrassing him."

* * * * * * *

The late Senator Ben (Pitchfork) Tillman of South Carolina is credited with having said:

"Texas has more trees and less timber; more rivers and less water; more resources and less cash; more itinerant preachers and less religion; more cows and less milk, and you can see farther and see less than any d—— country in the world."

* * * * * * *

Some idea of the size of Texas may be gained from the story of the traveling man, representing a house in Kansas City, who reported that he had arrived in El Paso (on the western rim of Texas), whereupon his manager telegraphed, "Now that you're in Texas run over to Texarkana and collect that old account." Since Texarkana is on the very eastern edge, the traveling man wired back, "Run over there and collect it yourself; you're closer than I am."

* * * * * * *

What's the matter with Texas?

The Texas farmer gets up to the sound of a Connecticut alarm clock, puts on a pair of overalls made in Detroit, washes his face in a Pittsburgh basin with Cincinnati soap, dries on a towel made in New Hampshire, eats Kansas City bacon and Indiana grits fried in Omaha lard and cooked on a Kalamazoo stove, buys Irish potatoes grown in Idaho and canned fruits put up in California, hitches his Missouri mule, fed on Iowa corn, to an Illinois plow, works all day, then crawls under a New Jersey blanket and is kept awake all night by the howling of a dog—the only home product on the whole durn place.

3

God's Country!

Yes, He couldn't give it to anybody so He had to keep it Himself.

* * * * * * *

Texas—where men are men and women are glad of it.

* * * * * * *

Is Texas big?

Why it's so big that the people living in El Paso (at the western extremity) refer to those at Texarkana as "effete Easterners" and the citizens away down south at Brownsville speak of the inhabitants of Dallas as "damyankees."

* * * * * * *

Texans seldom "knock" other states—though one was heard to remark that California is too far from Texas ever to amount to very much; and a talkative Kentuckian evoked the comment, "Kentucky? Ain't that where a fellow is 17 years old before his feet touch the ground because he's roostin' up in a tree, watchin' for revenuers?"

* * * * * * *

A bit of hitherto unpublished history:

On the way to Texas, the roads divided, one leading to Arkansas, the other to this State. The latter route bore a sign: "This road to Texas."

All who could read came to Texas; the others settled in Arkansas.

* * * * * * *

A teacher called on a new pupil from the East to tell about the Alamo.

"That's pie with ice cream," the boy said.

* * * * * * *

In the early days in the Panhandle, a man was driving along the road in a buggy at a high rate of speed. A friend ran out, flagged him down and asked why he was driving so rapidly.

"Well, it's like this," the other responded. "You know I own two sections of land up here and this morning I sold one of them to that greenhorn from Ohio and, while he wasn't looking, I slipped the other section into the deed and I'm leaving in a hurry before he finds out the trick I played him."

* * * * * * *

Parts of far West Texas were created just to hold the rest of the world together, says R. K. Phillips, Weatherford publisher.

4

Out on the plains, a citizen will gaze down the railroad track and then remark:

"Number Nine is due in thirty minutes and I can't see it yet; must be running behind time."

* * * * * * *

A visitor who had to ride one of the little rail lines in order to reach a small Texas town where a friend lived complained about the slowness of the trains.

"That's one way to look at it," the Texan agreed, "but think how long you get to ride for a dollar."

* * * * * * *

There was a little oil field line between Cisco and Breckenridge where you got to ride 90 miles for a 30-mile fare—30 miles up, 30 miles down and 30 miles forward.

* * * * * * *

The first train was crossing the Texas plains and a buffalo came charging down the track straight at the locomotive. The engineer exclaimed:

"Old fellow, I admire your nerve but durn your judgment!"

* * * * * * *

A boy going to town to see the first train ever to enter the place was walking along the track when he saw the train coming up behind him. He broke into a run, right down the track, and barely kept in the lead till the station was reached. Somebody asked him:

"Why didn't you get off the track?"

To which he replied:

"Ef I'd a got over there in that plowed ground, it would a caught me sure."

* * * * * * *

General Sheridan is credited with having declared:

"If I owned hell and Texas, I'd rent out Texas and live in hell."

* * * * * * *

There was a cowboy who had the Lord's Prayer framed and hung on the wall; then each night, just before he dived under the covers, he would point to it and say, "Oh, Lord, them's my sentiments."

5

WEATHER

"Nobody but fools and newcomers predict the weather in Texas."

* * * * * * *

Someone—having rashly prophesied the weather—was reminded of the fools'—and—newcomers' saying. Replied he:

"Come to think of it, they're the only two classes of people I've seen in the State."

* * * * * * *

A drouth became so severe that the preacher suggested a meeting be held to pray for rain. Old Timer remarked, "Go ahead if you want to, but prayin' ain't gonna do you a bit o' good unless the wind's outa the east."

* * * * * * *

An inhabitant of far West Texas said sadly:

"I wish it would rain—not for my sake because I've seen it rain but on account of my seven-year-old boy."

6

Oh, it's dusty out here in West Texas,
In the land where the strong breezes blow,
And the ranches go by in handfuls—
Where they come from, you never know.
You can go to the cellar or attic,
Or even get under the bed,
But still you'll get dust in your gizzard,
In your ears, and on top of your head.

Oh, it's dusty out here in West Texas—
We wonder how long it will blow.
We surely must like this country:
We have to eat it, you know.
There's gray sand and black dirt in fistfuls,
Sailing around in the sky;
So here's a toast to West Texas
And a slogan: "Here's mud in your eye!"

* * * * * * *

The Secretary of a Chamber of Commerce was writing a letter to Washington asking for drouth relief when he suddenly found water was lapping around his ankles: a sudden freshet had caused the banks of the creek that ran through the town to overflow. His poise wasn't shaken for a moment; he just crossed out "drouth" and wrote "flood."

* * * * * * *

Rain? There was a barrel laying on the ground with both ends out and it rained so hard that the water went in the bung-hole faster than it could run out at both ends.

* * * * * * *

An Easterner remarked to a native:
"Awfully rainy weather—like the Flood."
The cowboy repeated, doubtfully:
"The Flood?"
The stranger said:
"The Flood—Noah, the Ark, Mount Ararat."
The cowboy shook his head:
"I ain't seen the paper yet this morning."

* * * * * * *

A farmer set out for town in a wagon drawn by a yoke of oxen. On the way, one of the oxen died of sunstroke and, as he was skinning the animal, the other one froze to death.

7

Texas—where it's 100 in the shade, and no shade.

* * * * * * *

A West Texas rain: a sandstorm.

* * * * * * *

And speaking of sandstorms:

A farmer applied to his banker for a loan. The banker said, "I'll have to go out and inspect your place first."

The farmer replied, "That won't be necessary; here comes the farm now."

* * * * * * *

A cowpuncher wanted some warm water for shaving one morning. Before he noticed, the kettle was boiling so he set it outside the ranchhouse to cool. Two minutes later, it had frozen —and had frozen so quickly that the ice was still warm!

* * * * * * *

Away up on the plains in the Texas Panhandle is the city of Amarillo, 3,500 feet above sea-level. An old saying is:

"There's nothing between Amarillo and the North Pole except a barbed wire fence."

* * * * * * *

And when it's especially cold, say, around Austin, down in the middle of Texas, you are sure to hear the remark:

"Somebody musta tore down Amarillo's fence."

* * * * * * *

It is said that when Admiral Peary reached the North Pole, he remarked:

"Gee, I'll bet it's cold in Amarillo this morning."

* * * * * * *

They have a wind gauge up near Amarillo. It consists of a fence post to which a boulder is anchored by a chain. When a gale comes along with sufficient power to lift the boulder straight out in the air at the end of the chain, natives remark:

"Well, the wind is blowing today."

* * * * * * *

"Does the wind blow like this all the time out here?" a traveler asked at a West Texas filling station.

"No, sir; sometimes it turns around and blows the other way," was the reply.

A different version:

As a heavy wind was whistling through the little town a visitor asked, "Does the wind blow like this all the time?"

A native replied, "No, sometimes it blows like h——."

* * * * * * *

However, there is one area in West Texas where the wind is so mild that there isn't enough to turn all the windmills at one time—so they run half of them a while and then the other half.

* * * * * * *

One balmy morning, a farmer tossed a dipper of water at a cat. A norther struck as the water was in mid-air, freezing it, and the chunk of ice broke the cat's skull.

* * * * * * *

When a man's hat blows off, he telegraphs to the station ahead.

Or (another version) he just reaches up and pulls down another hat.

It is recorded that a high wind once blew a cookstove twenty miles and, next day, came back for the kettle and the wood-box.

And another time the wind was so strong that a stranger who was knock-kneed became bow-legged in two days.

* * * * * * *

During a sandstorm, a prairie dog has been seen digging a hole forty feet in the air.

(This sight can no longer be witnessed, however—as prairie dogs are practically extinct in Texas.)

* * * * * * *

One veracious observer relates that during a sandstorm he saw a prairie dog digging straight up, trying to get a breath of air.

* * * * * * *

An Englishman was riding with a cowboy when they entered a canyon and a sudden gust of wind blew the Britisher to the ground. He arose and said:

"I say but you rawther overdo the ventilation out here."

* * * * * * *

A citizen of the Panhandle who went down into the Magic Valley of Texas, some 800 miles south, in April sent a telegram back home:

"S. O. S.; B. V. D.; P. D. Q."

9

"Do you ever have cyclones up here?" a visitor in West Texas asked.

"No, sir-e-e," he was informed. "We did have one once but it ran into a sandstorm about three miles out of town and was ripped to pieces."

* * * * * * *

During one rather severe sandstorm a man was seen driving a combine at a high rate of speed down the road. In response to a question, he explained:

"I planted wheat and I'm gonna harvest it if I have to chase it all the way to the Gulf of Mexico."

* * * * * * *

A traveler going through a little town in Southwest Texas saw a teacher on the school campus with a group of little children. She had a garden hose and as the water sparkled through the air, she said:

"Boys and girls, that's what rain looks like."

* * * * * * *

After the flood hit Galveston some forty years ago, causing great loss of life, one of the victims—newly arrived in heaven—was telling others about the disaster but, right in the midst of the story, one of the listeners yawned and walked away.

The Texans asked: "Who was that old so-and-so with a long gray beard and wearing a kimono who was so bored?"

"Oh, that was Noah," another said.

* * * * * * *

George was from Arkansas and he grew home-sick out in the barren, sandy spaces of far West Texas. So he sent back to Marked Tree for a baby bull-frog as a memento of the region he had left behind. George reared the creature with the greatest care and, water being scarce, he gradually accustomed the frog to spend more and more time out of his natural element until at last Bosco (as he had named the pet) ceased to yearn for the moistrue of the swamps and became contented with dry land.

One day, George was called away and had to leave Bosco alone. Returning late in the afternoon, George was oppressed with the sense of impending tragedy. There hung about the little adobe house in its setting of cactus and mesquite the same dark atmosphere that surrounded the House of Usher. And, in the living room, George found his worst fears realized.

Bosco had fallen into a pitcher of water and had drowned!

"Is it hot in West Texas?" the traveling man in the Beaumont hotel lobby repeated the question.

"Why, I was out there last week and I saw a coyote chasing a jack-rabbit—and it was so hot, they were both walking."

* * * * * * *

A motorist, stopping for gas, and water in a town in the Big Bend country, remarked:

"Nice town you have here."

The young attendant snorted:

"It's hotter'n h—— in the Summer and liable to drop forty degrees in three hours in the Winter and the wind blows all the time."

The visitor replied:

"Well, I guess the people are all right, anyway."

"Naw, they're the oneriest, triflin'est folks you can find anywhere."

Nettled, the autoist said:

"Well, except for the climate and the people, I guess you could say the town is all right."

"Yes," answered the boy, "and you could say the same thing about h——."

* * * * * * *

There was a noted individual named Fishback who used to live over near Sulphur River from which he hauled water in a barrel on a slide drawn by a horse, the traces of the harness being made of rawhide.

One day, he had just filled the barrel when a sudden rain came up and he took refuge in a hollow tree until it was over. As he started home, Fishback noticed that the horse was pulling with difficulty but he ascribed it to the slippery condition of the ground.

Upon reaching the cabin, he found that the slide was not in sight. Fishback, however, was not disturbed as there was sufficient water in the rain-barrel, as the result of the shower, for the night; and he would go back for the sled next morning.

So he slipped collar, hames and traces off the animal, hung them on a stump, then went into the house where he had a cup of coffee (or maybe something a mite stronger) and when he came to the door, a strange sight greeted him: the slide with the barrel on it was coming slowly up the hill. The rawhide traces had stretched because of the rain but, when the sun had come out again, the heat drew them up!

11

The vagaries of Texas weather are illustrated by the experience of a hunter who told of seeing thousands of ducks on a lake. As he raised his gun to fire, a norther struck, freezing the water. At the roar of the gun, the ducks flew away, carrying the lake with them.

* * * * * * *

The waitress placed a bowl of chicken soup in front of Sagebrush Sam, then—glancing outside—she remarked:
"Looks like rain."
Not lifting his eyes, Sam said:
"Tastes like it, too."

* * * * * * *

Out in the semi-arid region, the sight of rain caused a man to faint.
Bystanders revived him by throwing sand in his face.

* * * * * * *

A settler built a cabin and lived there for ten years. All that time, he hauled water in barrels from a creek, some six miles away. At last he sold the place and as the new owner was about to take possession, he was astonished to see the seller dipping water out of a barrel and throwing it up on the house. When an explanation was demanded, the settler said:
"I always have wanted to know if that roof would leak."

* * * * * * *

HELL IN TEXAS

The devil, we're told, in hell was chained,
And a thousand years he there remained;
He never complained nor did he groan,
But determined to start a hell of his own,
Where he could torment the souls of men
Without being chained in a prison pen.
So he asked the Lord if He had on hand
Anything left when He made the land.

The Lord said, "Yes, I had plenty on hand,
But I left it down on the Rio Grande;
The fact is, old boy, the stuff is so poor
I don't think you could use it in hell anymore."
But the devil went down to look at the truck,
And said if it came as a gift he was stuck;
For after examining it carefully and well
He concluded the place was too dry for hell.

So, in order to get it off His hands,
The Lord promised the devil to water the lands;
For He had some water, or rather some dregs,
A regular cathartic that smelled like bad eggs.
Hence the deal was closed and the deed was given
And the Lord went back to His home in heaven.
And the devil then said, "I have all that is needed
To make a good hell," and hence he succeeded.

He began to put thorns in all of the trees,
And mixed up the sand with millions of fleas;
And scattered tarantulas along all the roads;
Put thorns on the cactus and horns on the toads.
He lengthened the horns of the Texas steers,
And put an addition on the rabbit's ears;
He put a little devil in the broncho steed,
And poisoned the feet of the centipede.

The rattlesnake bites you, the scorpion stings,
The mosquito delights you with his buzzing wings;
The sand-burrs prevail and so do the ants,
And those who sit down need half-soles on their pants.
The devil then said that throughout the land
He'd managed to keep up the devil's own brand,
And all would be mavericks unless they bore
The marks of scratches and bites and thorns by the score.

The heat in the summer is a hundred and ten,
Too hot for the devil and too hot for men.
The wild boar roams through the black chaparral,—
It's a hell of a place he has for a hell.
The red pepper grows on the banks of the brook;
The Mexicans use it in all that they cook.
Just dine with a Greaser and then you will shout,
"I've hell on the inside as well as the out!"

*   *   *   *   *   *   *

During an extra heavy windstorm, a soldier came floating through the air and landed in an Army camp in far West Texas. A captain said, "What you mean doing parachute practice during such a wind as this?" The soldier said, "I didn't come down in a parachute, sir; I went up in a tent."

13

LONE
PRAIRIE-E-E

I'm from Texas; you can't steer me.

*   *   *   *   *   *   *

A newcomer to Texas was so green that he thought you had to have a gun to shoot craps.

He thought a dogie was something you built houses out of.

And that a lasso was a girl—and remuda was some sort of grass.

Why, he even thought a cowboy was a bull.

*   *   *   *   *   *   *

A tough hombre called for a glass of half-and-half—half milk and half whisky. As he was drinking it, a "tenderfoot" preacher walked in and seeing a customer drinking what appeared to be a glass of milk, said:

"One of the same."

He took a sip, blinked his eyes, took another sip, then gulped the entire contents down, smacked his lips and exclaimed:

"Brother, what a cow!"

Dogie—a calf whose mammy has died and whose pappy has run off with another cow.

* * * * * * *

A group of hunters, tired and hungry, applied for food and shelter at a one-room cabin. The old-timer, after a supper of salt pork, corn-bread and molasses. said:

"Two of you can sleep on that corn-shuck mattress on the floor; and the others will just have to rough it."

* * * * * * *

The cowboys on one ranch got tired of plain fare so they sent one of their number to town for some good grub. He came back with ten quarts of whisky and a loaf of bread; and they sure were mad.

"What are we goin' to do with all that bread?" they demanded.

* * * * * * *

A middle-aged West Texas ranchman, suddenly rich from oil, bought a limousine and—as he didn't know how to drive—employed a liveried chauffeur. A few weeks later, the chauffeur eloped with the rancher's wife and the car. Now every time the poor ranchman hears a car honk, he almost has a breakdown—afraid it's the chauffeur bringing his wife back.

* * * * * * *

A fellow boasted:

"I'm so tough I can climb a thorn-tree back'ards with a wildcat under each arm and never get a scratch."

When he showed up, with his face badly scratched, the boaster was reminded that he said he could climb a thorn-tree with a load of wild-cats and not get a mark. But he was ready with an explanation:

"I got these scratches climbin' down."

* * * * * * *

J. Frank Dobie, authority on the lore of the Longhorn, tells an amusing story about cattle brands.

A ranchman branded his cattle "I C"—whereupon an enterprising individual who decided to go into busines for himself began branding the first man's cattle "I C U." But the rightful owner was not to be out-smarted. He adopted a new brand:

"I C U 2."

A farmer who was born near the little town of Dothan, in the western edge of Eastland County, and had spent all his life in that vicinity was summoned for jury duty in federal court at Abilene, some 45 miles on west. When he returned to Dothan he told his cronies:

"If the world is as big in the other directions as it is on the west, it's a mighty big place."

* * * * * * *

A traveler in the most forlorn portion of Western Texas entered a little cafe run in conjunction with a store and filling station.

"What do you have?" he asked.

"Mainly canned goods," the waiter said.

"Can't you do better than that?" the customer persisted.

"Well, I could go out and catch a sage-hen."

"Does it have wings?" the visitor asked.

"Yes."

"Does it have legs?"

"Yes."

"Then give me something out of a can; anything that has wings and legs and won't leave this country would be too tough for me."

* * * * * * *

Four Panhandle cowpunchers, tired of hard tack and beans, meandered into a Canadian (Texas) cafe.

The first one said, "Gimme a double order of beefsteak and make it rare."

Said the second, "Double that and make it rarer."

From the third one, "Singe a shoulder and bring it in."

The last one began slowly whetting his pocket-knife and drawled:

"Jest cripple a calf and drive 'im by. I'll get mine!"

* * * * * * *

Different, however, was a cowboy who went into a Dallas restaurant and ordered a steak, well done.

The waitress brought in the steak, set it before him but when the cowboy began to carve, he let out a yell:

"You call that well-done! In my country, I've seen cows cut worse than that get well."

Nobody wanted to be cook in the cow-camp. Lots were drawn but with the understanding that the first to find fault would have to take over the cooking duties.

All went well for a few days. Then one of the cowpunchers, forgetting the agreement, said:

"These are the d—dest biscuits I ever ate!"

Then, recalling the compact, he hastily added:

"But I sure do like 'em!"

* * * * * * *

The train stopped ten minutes for lunch but the waitress was overwhelmed by the orders and it looked as though one of the passengers, a young woman, was going to have to return to the train without drinking even a cup of coffee as the beverage served her was steaming hot.

A gallant cowboy said:

"Here, ma'am, take mine, it's already been saucered and blowed."

* * * * * * *

I've rode a pitchin' bronc till the sky was underneath;
I've tackled every desert in the land;
I've sampled whiskey till I couldn't hardly see,
An' dallied with the quicksands of the Grande;
I've argued with the marshals of half-a-dozen burgs;
I've been dragged free and fancy by a cow;
I've had three years' campaignin' with fightin',
    bitin' Ninth,
And I never lost my temper till right now.
I've had the yellow fever and been shot plum full o'
    holes;
I've grabbed an army mule by the tail;
But I've never been so snortin', really hifalutin' mad
As when you up and hands me ginger ale.

* * * * * * *

Then there was a the cowboy who was feeling so happy, he shouted:

"I can whip a rattlesnake and give 'im the first bite!"

* * * * * * *

The International & Great Northern Railroad runs through the southwestern part of Texas. A cowboy looked at the lettering "I & G N" painted on the locomotive and remarked:

"Ain't that a durn funny way to spell injun?"

17

Of course, most famous of all stories about ranchmen is the one about the cattle king who visited New York City, couldn't read the French on the menu in the fashionable restaurant and bellowed:

"Bring me twenty-five dollars worth of ham and eggs."

* * * * * * *

The magnitude of the ranch of the late W. T. Waggoner, reputed to have been the richest man west of the Mississippi River, is illustrated by this story:

Two men were talking and, when one of them mentioned a county, the other asked:

"Where is that?"

The other answered, "Oh, it's one of the counties on Tom Waggoner's ranch."

* * * * * * *

"The corn crop was sorter short one year," a farmboy related. "We had corn for dinner one day and paw ate fourteen acres of it."

* * * * * * *

Out in a stretch of dreary, sandy country, a settler was having such a hard time that he decided to try to get a loan on his land. When the appraiser came out, the settler handed over the deed and abstract for inspection and then they set out in a car to look the place over.

It was a melancholy sight but suddenly the visitor's face lighted up as he caught sight of a prairie dog. As the automobile approached, the prairie dog popped out of sight in the hole but the appraiser walked on over, tossed the deed and abstract into the hole and started kicking dirt and rocks into the opening.

"What in the world!" exclaimed the settler.

"Anything that can make a living on this land deserves title to it," the other explained.

* * * * * * *

Farms are so big in Texas that on one of them a man starts out in the Spring and plows a straight furrow right on through until Fall and then he harvests back.

On the biggest farms, a young married couple will go out to milk the cows and their children come back with the milk.

There was one farm that had such a big crop that they stacked all the wheat out-of-doors that there was room for and then put the rest in the barn.

Pious Pete was regaling a bunch of tenderfeet on the dude ranch one night around the campfire with stories of his adventures on the range.

"Most excitin' adventure I ever had was in the mountains in the Big Bend country," he related. "I was walkin' along a ledge on the side of a mountain when I turned a corner an' there was a loafer (a lobo). Well, I didn't have my gun so I just began backin'—the ledge was too narrow fer me to turn aroun' an' the big wolf came snarlin' along.

"I happened to look in the direction I was backin' and there was a mountain lion blockin' the path—and it was 900 feet straight down and it was impossible for me to scale the solid rock wall.

"An' at the same instant, both of them varmints crouched to spring at me."

Excitedly, one of the listeners said:

"How did you escape?"

"Oh, I didn't; I lost my life and the biggest regret of it all is that I never knew which got me—the wolf or the mountain lion."

And that ended the session.

*   *   *   *   *   *   *

A half-drunken "bad man" entered a railroad coach, flourished a six-gun in each hand and bellowed:

"I'm gonna rob every man on this hyah train and I'm gonna kiss every woman."

A determined-looking ranchman arose and said:

"Pardner, you can rob us men but durned ef you're gonna kiss the ladies."

An old maid said to the rancher:

"You leave that man alone; *he's* a-robbin' this train."

*   *   *   *   *   *   *

A traveling preacher conducting a meeting out in West Texas said:

"All Christians please stand."

No one arose and he exclaimed:

"What! Not a single friend of Jesus in the house!"

At this a cowboy got up with the remark:

"Stranger, I don't know who this man Jesus is but I'll stand up for any man that hasn't got any more friends than He has."

19

The herds of some of the early-day cattlemen in Texas increased rapidly, perhaps by branding animals belonging to others. Of such a ranchman, it might be remarked, "His cows always have twin calves."

The habit of such men, when they needed meat, of butchering a "critter" belonging to somebody else, gave rise to the remark:

"He never tasted any of his own beef until one day he accidentally ate some in another man's camp."

* * * * * * *

A tenderfoot, watching a poker game, turned to a cowboy and whispered excitedly:

"Did you see him slip the ace from the bottom of the deck?"

To which the other calmly answered:

"Wall, it was his deal, wasn't it?"

* * * * * * *

A cowboy was telling another about a speech he'd heard and he fell back on a range metaphor. Having in mind the wide-spreading horns of a Longhorn, the cow-puncher said:

"The speech had two points a long ways apart with a lot of bull in between."

* * * * * * *

The foreman of a famous, old-time West Texas rancher was testifying on behalf of his employer. The cross-examining lawyer demanded:

"You're Tom Waggoner's man Friday, aren't you?"

Without batting an eye, the loyal foreman replied:

"Yes, sir, I'm his man Friday; also Saturday, Sunday, Monday, Tuesday, Wednesday and Thursday; I'm his man all the time."

* * * * * * *

A cowboy in town wandered into church one Sunday morning and was so impressed by the service that he threw a five-dollar bill into the collection plate.

At the door as the congregation was filing out, the minister said:

"I hope you enjoyed the sermon."

"Yes, sir, parson," the cowboy replied, "I put five dollars in the plate and you know that's a h—— of a lot of money."

To which the sky-pilot countered, "Yes, but I'm a d—— good preacher."

A bunch of the boys were sitting around a campfire out on the range.

Conversation lagged among the nine cowpunchers. Finally, one spoke up:

"Let's all tell our names before we came to Texas."

Eight pistols rang out as one . . .

There was another grave on the lone prairie.

* * * * * * *

On a dude ranch, a tenderfoot said:

"I've never ridden a horse so maybe you'd better give me one that hasn't ever been ridden—so we can start even."

* * * * * * *

A herd stampeded and the cowboy decided that the only way to stop the cattle was to head them off.

Ahead of him, however, was a canyon, a thousand feet deep and a hundred feet wide.

Dismounting, he led "Old Paint" to the brink so he could size it up, then they went back a hundred yards to develop speed.

Horse and rider took off into space. Twenty feet out—going fine; fifty feet out—still going fine; sixty feet—"Old Paint" began to weaken; seventy-five feet saw he couldn't make it—turned around and came back.

* * * * * * *

A similar adventure:

A cowboy and horse traveling through heavy darkness fell into a canyon 500 feet deep. As they were plunging through space the cowboy yelled, "Whoa" and the horse was so well trained that he stopped just 10 feet from the ground.

* * * * * * *

A cowboy, visiting a city for the first time, registered at a hotel.

"Do you want to leave a call?" the clerk asked.

"No. I'll just sleep on through till daylight," the cowboy replied.

* * * * * * *

A West Texas cattleman, waking up in a Fort Worth hotel after a big celebration the night before, drained a pitcher of ice water at one draught and then said:

"If I'd a-known water tasted so good, I'd a-dug a well a long time ago."

A group of friends in an El Paso saloon were playing a new game—Question and Answer. If anybody asked a question and someone else answered it, the questioner had to buy a round of drinks. But if nobody could answer it, they all had to buy him a drink—provided he could answer his own question.

One merrymaker propounded this interrogatory:

"How is it that a prairie dog can dig a hole fifty feet deep and leave no dirt on the outside?"

They all gave up so he triumphantly said:

"The prairie dog don't leave any dirt on the outside because he starts at the bottom and digs up."

There was a silence, then someone asked:

"But how does he get to the bottom to start digging?"

"Ah," said the first man, "that's your question—you answer it."

* * * * * * *

Overtaken by night, a cowboy hitched his horse to a bush on top of a hill and rolled up in his blanket at the foot of the hill.

Next morning, the hill had vanished and the horse had disappeared.

Magically, though, there was a tree nearby that had not been there when he went to sleep.

Looking up, he saw in the top branches, forty feet above the ground, his horse.

Then he realized what had happened. The hill had been merely a mound of sand piled up by a wind. During the night, another wind had come along, blowing away the sand and exposing the tree, whose top he had mistaken for a bush.

* * * * * * *

Equally remarkable was the experience of a cowboy who decided to take a swim in a pool at the foot of a cliff.

He took off his clothes, but just as he dived, a sandstorm sucked the pool dry. Plunging through space, he had the horrible thought that he would be dashed to pieces on the rocky bed but, just before he struck, a cloudburst arrived, refilled the pool and he enjoyed a nice swim.

* * * * * * *

A cowboy asked a visitor on a "dude" ranch, "What kind of saddle do you want—one with a horn or one without?"

The tenderfoot replied, "Without, I guess; there doesn't seem to be much traffic on these prairies."

22

An Englishman who was indulging in boasting aroused the ire of a grizzled rancher.

"Queen Victoria touched my grandfather on the shoulder with a sword and made a lord out of him," the Londoner said.

"That's nothing," the ranchman snorted. "Old Geronimo touched my grandpa on the head with a tomahawk and made an angel out of him."

* * * * * * *

J. Frank Dobie, most celebrated of living Texas authors, tells a story of an Englishman who decided to go into the ranching business. He announced he was going to buy several thousand head of cattle but he intended to be sure that nothing was put over on him and so he was going to count the animals personally. The ranchman who was selling him the cattle took up his station with the Englishman near a hill and then the foreman drove the animals around and around this hill, the tenderfoot buying the same ones over and over again. There was one tobacco-colored steer with an oddly-shaped horn and after he had been by three times, the Englishman commented:

"I never saw so many steers with such odd coloring and horns"—so the ranchman quietly gave instructions to the foreman to drive the steer clear away. However, the animal returned and took up the parade but the Britisher suspected nothing and paid for the cattle.

That night, the ranchman heard a noise and investigated. It was that old steer, still going around and around that hill and he kept it up for four days and nights until he finally fell over and died of exhaustion.

* * * * * * *

Another story that Dobie relates is about a cowboy with a wonderful horse. Riding along in the pitch darkness, horse and rider plunged off into space.

"It was so far down," the cowboy used to narrate, "that I had time to roll a cigaret, light it and take three draws before we hit with a terrible jolt. Ole Dan just stood there even after I'd spoke to him several times. This was so unlike him, he bein' so obedient that I decided to investigate.

"So I got down and found that he had bogged up to his knees in granite."

23

A newcomer who wanted to establish a ranch—this was just recently—had a hard time finding a brand that was not already registered. His cattle were very bad about straying on the highway, which was near his land, and one day he saw a cow staring at a road sign with an arrow on it, meaning "Right turn."

So that gave him an idea and he recorded as his brand a "Right turn" arrow and also a "Left turn" arrow.

When round-up time came for branding and marking, the new cattleman noticed that the animals were going around and around the fence in the 500-acre pasture in which they were confined. He saddled his horse and rode through the herd and discovered that, since the critters had practically been raised on the highway, they knew the meaning of the two signs and all the ones branded "Right turn" were going one way and all the "Left turn" ones were going the other—

All except one yearling that had got an eye hurt and he was in the wrong gang!

* * * * * * *

A revenue officer called at a mountain cabin and found no one there but a boy. The following conversation ensued:

"Where's your father?"
"Pappy's at the still."
'Where's your mother?"
"Maw's at the still."
"Where's your brothers and sisters?"
"They're at the still."
"I'll give you a dollar to take me to the still."
"Gimme the dollar."
"I'll give it to you when I get back."
"Mister, you ain't comin' back."

* * * * * * *

A cowboy, who was somewhat under the influence of liquor, climbed into a carriage in a funeral procession of a complete stranger to him and rode to the cemetery. There he took a seat and was asleep until the minister announced the text:

"The Lord giveth and the Lord taketh away."

Rousing up, the cowboy exclaimed, "That's a d—— fair proposition an' I'll lick anybody in the crowd that says it ain't."

Many years ago, a guest at a Texas hotel said to the clerk:
"Have the porter bring down my baggage."
"What is your baggage?" the clerk asked.
"A Bowie knife, two pistols, a deck of cards and a shirt," was
the reply.

* * * * * * *

Bob McFall, sheriff during the Burkburnett oil boom, says
that in his cow punching days one of his associates said he was
going to move to a place where everything started with a "p":
"To Palo Pinto; build me a pine-pole pen, raise pigs, pos-
sums, porcupines, and pumpkins; drink pot licker and ride a
pacing pony."

* * * * * * *

One thinly-inhabited county was famous for its stills. When
one saw thin blue wisps rising from the thickets, the remark
would be made:
"Those are smoke from our factories."

* * * * * * *

The "strong, silent men" of the "great open spaces" are a
tradition. Two such men lived in a one-room shack and had
"batched" there for years. One evening, after supper, they heard
a sound off in the woods and one remarked, "Sounds like a bull
a-bellerin'." The other replied, "Sounds more like a steer."
They turned in and, next morning, the man who had made
the remark about it seeming like a steer awoke to find his
associate saddling up and getting ready to "pull out" for keeps.
"What's the matter?" he demanded of the departing one.
"Too d—— much argument," the other answered.

* * * * * * *

Inscription in Boot Hill cemetery:
"Played five aces.
Now playing a harp."
Another epitaph:
"Shoot-'em-up Jake
Ran for sheriff, 1872.
Ran from sheriff, 1876.
Buried, 1876."

25

The poker game was fast and furious. Suddenly, Pistol Pete yanked his six-shooter out and shouted:

"This game ain't honest! Alkali Ike ain't playin' the hand I dealt him."

* * * * * * *

Deceived by the clear atmosphere into thinking that a mountain in West Texas was near at hand, a tenderfoot set out to walk to it. After several hours however the peak was seemingly as far away as ever, so he turned around and walked back to the ranch house.

On another walk, this time with his host, the visitor—when they reached a very small stream—started peeling off his clothes.

Amazed, the Texan exclaimed, "You can jump this stream; what are you doing?"

The Easterner said, "I'm gonna swim it; I'm not gonna be fooled again."

* * * * * * *

An old-timer, speaking of the intelligence of women and the intelligence of cows, remarked:

"A crowd of women attending a bridge party brought their babies with them and placed them in an adjoining room. One of the youngsters let out a squawk and everyone of the mothers jumped up and ran to see if it was her offspring.

"But you can have a round-up of a thousand cows and calves and stand guard on them on a dark night, and one calf that has walked out to the edge of the herd can bawl, and one cow— and only one—will come out and claim it."

—Make your own application, if you dare.

* * * * * * *

All the teamsters of the wagon train, en route to California in the early days, would sleep under their wagons at night—all except "Tex." He would unroll his bedding out in the open. One of the others asked him, "Why don't you sleep under your wagon?" To which, Tex drawled:

"Too confining."

* * * * * * *

An Eastern professor on a Texas train, who found himself in company with an 81-year old cowboy, asked: "To what do you attribute your long life?" The Texan said, "Well, I never stole a hoss an' I never called a man a liar to his face."

26

LAW AND (Maybe) ORDER

A blustering, ignorant attorney was accustomed to ask a witness on cross-examination:

"Where wuz you at on the 27th of March, 1938, if anywhere?"

*   *   *   *   *   *   *

A judge in an Eastern state ruled that the mere fact that a wife shot at her husband one time was not sufficient grounds for divorce. In Texas when a wife shoots at her husband one time, he doesn't need a divorce.

*   *   *   *   *   *   *

"Do you have a criminal lawyer in Prickly Pear?"

"Yes—but we can't prove it on him."

*   *   *   *   *   *   *

Of Captain Bill McDonald, renowned Texas Ranger, it was said:

"He would charge h—— single-handed with a bucket of water."

27

A new adjutant general decided that reports and records of the Texas Rangers' activities should be more detailed and so a veteran Ranger captain, having killed an outlaw, was laboriously filling out one of the new-fangled printed forms.

He reached the section for stating what had been done with the case, the heading being "Disposition," and he wrote:

"Mean as h——."

*   *   *   *   *   *   *

"Tell us about the fight," a lawyer asked an elderly East Texas woman.

"I didn't see no fight," she replied.

"Well, tell us what you did see," said the attorney, leaning back lazily.

"I went to a dance over at the Turners' house," the woman said, "and as the men swung around and changed partners, they would slap each other and one fellow hit another one harder than the other one liked and so he hit back and somebody out with a knife and somebody else drew a six-shooter and another fellow out with a rifle that was under the bed and the air was full of yelling and smoke and bullets, and I saw there was going to be a fight, so I left."

*   *   *   *   *   *   *

"What caused his death?"

"Five aces."

*   *   *   *   *   *   *

A young attorney, addressing the Supreme Court of Texas at considerable length, happened to catch the chief justice in the middle of a yawn. In frigid tone, the barrister said:

"I trust I am not unduly intruding upon the time of this honorable court."

Stung by the remark, the chief justice rejoined:

"No—there is a difference between intruding upon the time of this honorable court, and encroaching on eternity."

*   *   *   *   *   *   *

A wealthy ranchman shot a man to death on the streets in a Panhandle city and then telegraphed to one of the leading criminal lawyers of the State, who lived in Fort Worth, three hundred miles away, offering a $5,000 fee.

The attorney telegraphed back:

"Am leaving for your town on next train, bringing three eye-witnesses."

The long, tall, loosed-jointed lawyer's middle initial was "N"—probably standing for "Necessity" because "Necessity knows no law." Anyway, he stood before the judge in federal court and said:

"Good judge, your honor, you will have to postpone this case a couple of days."

The judge bristled:

"This court doesn't have to postpone any case."

"Yes, but good judge, your honor," the attorney continued, "you'll have to postpone this one for two days."

"Why?" barked his honor.

"Because the lady who is the defendant in this case became a mother this morning."

"Well—" spluttered the judge, "well—do you think two days is a long enough continuance?"

"Oh, I think so; it was a mighty little baby." . . . .

When the case came up, the proof showed that the woman had a quantity of non-tax paid liquor. Her attorney pleaded:

"She had this whisky to fortify her against the ordeal of approaching motherhood."

"Yes," said the judge, "but she had 50 gallons. Don't you think that's a large amount of whisky for an expectant mother?"

"I don't know, good judge, your honor," answered the attorney, "because I never was an expectant mother."

* * * * * * *

Texarkana is divided by the boundary line of Texas and Arkansas.

Back in early days, so it is related, legal procedure was rather confusing when an offender was brought before the judge, he was given his choice as to whether he would be tried under Texas or Arkansas law.

A man, who faced two charges (one of horse-theft and another of murder) said he preferred to stand trial under Arkansas statutes. The jury fined him $10 for stealing the horse but sentenced him to hang for killing the man—whereupon, the defendant said he had changed his mind and wanted to face trial under Texas law. His request was granted and the jury fined him $10 for the murder but condemned him to hang for stealing the horse!

* * * * * * *

"Gentlemen of the jury," an eloquent Texas barrister said, "I would not exchange my birthright for a mess of potash."

The lawyer represented two defendants who were on trial in the same case in United States district court.

"Gentlemen of the jury," he began, "I represent the Defendant Brown and the Defendant Smith and I would like to take up their defenses separately.

"First, let us discuss the Defendant Brown. When our forefathers came to this land, fleeing from persecution, they set up a government of the people, by the people and for the people. They ordained that every man was entitled to life, liberty and the pursuit of happiness.

"They decreed that every defendant was due his day in court; that he should have the right to be confronted by the witnesses against him and the right, also, to be represented by counsel of his own choosing; and further that there should be flung about his shoulders, like a mantle, the presumption of innocence until his guilt was established beyond a reasonable doubt.

"So much for the Defendant Brown. I will now take up the Defendant Smith—"

* * * * * * *

In a little town, the blacksmith killed a man. The citizens hung a shoemaker for the crime because they had two shoemakers but only one blacksmith.

* * * * * * *

And that calls to mind the brilliant young attorney who made his first argument before the higher tribunal in Texas. His address was filled with allusions to the Dred Scott decision, the rule in Shelley's case, Milton's "Areopagitica" and many another treasure of law and literature.

At the conclusion, the chief justice warmly congratulated the beaming lawyer from the bench and added:

"We have greatly enjoyed all the points you have brought out, and, if we ever have a case in which they are involved, we will bear in mind what you have said."

* * * * * * *

An Eastland County woman whose husband had died intestate wrote the following letter to Judge Joe Jones of the probate court:

"Dear Judge of the reprobate court:

"My husband died detested, leaving me with four little infidels and I want to be appointed their executioner."

The prisoner was accused of having stolen a horse. Not many years before, he would have received summary justice at the hands of cowboys but law and order had invaded West Texas, so he was on trial.

His lawyer made an eloquent speech, asserted that all the evidence was circumstantial and that anyone could gaze into the open, frank, honest face of the prisoner at the bar and see that he was as innocent as a new-born babe, as clean as a hound's tooth, as pure as the driven snow.

The jury returned a verdict of acquittal and the defendant, turning to his attorney, asked:

"Does that mean I get to keep the horse?"

* * * * * * *

A city was threatened by mob violence, so a telegram was sent to the governor to rush a force of Texas Rangers to the scene.

When the train arrived, a delegation was on hand to welcome the Rangers. A lone, leathery-cheeked big-hatted, high-booted, keen-eyed individual alighted. It was apparent that he was a Ranger but the citizens were disappointed and the spokesman said:

"Did the governor send only one Ranger?"

"H——, there ain't but one mob, is there?" he asked.

* * * * * * *

When Joe Jones handed a campaign card to a boy, the latter said:

"I'm not old enough to vote."

Jones answered:

"You will be before I quit running for office."

* * * * * * *

Joe Jones, who is still young but bids fair to become a legend soon, tells this one on himself:

It was my first big case and the judge announced that two hours would be allowed for argument to each side.

I said to an older attorney:

"I don't believe I know enough things to talk about to make a speech that long. Do I have to speak for the full two hours?"

He replied:

"No, but the longer you talk, the longer it'll be before your client starts for the penitentiary."

A little man was standing at a bar when a new arrival, a big, black-mustached fellow, jostled him. Quick as a flash, the small chap yanked out a six-shooter and said:

"When the Lord created men, He made some little and some big but when Colonel Colt made his invention, he made all men equal. Move over, you big blankety-blank!"

And he moved over.

* * * * * * *

The still was an enormous one and had been running for a good while. It seemed that federal officers stationed in Texas were unable to locate it but when "revenuers" were brought in from the East, they swooped down and rounded up a dozen men and women, seized several hundred gallons of whiskey and several thousand gallons of mash.

All this, the first government man testified to—but he wasn't sure whether the still was in Van Zandt County or over the line in the county to the east. And this was a vital point because the United States District Court sitting in Dallas had jurisdiction only far enough east to take in Van Zandt County.

The second and the third of the raiders testified to the same thing—the still, the whisky, the mash, the operatives, but neither witness knew in which county the "industry" was located.

"The Government rests," announced the assistant district attorney.

"What!" exclaimed the judge, for venue was unproved. "The jury is instructed to return a verdict of not guilty. The gentleman in the left-hand corner chair in the front row will sign the verdict as foreman."

"Take the stand, Sally Ann," said the defense attorney.

"No, you won't take the stand, Sally Ann; you are all free of the charge; Mr. Attorney, take your clients and get out of the courtroom," said the judge, angry at the miscarriage of justice.

Outside, newspapermen asked the lawyer if he had been surprised at the instructed verdict.

"No," the barrister replied, "I knew that good judge wouldn't believe them d——, lyin', blue-bellied Yankees!"

* * * * * * *

Asked if he knew a certain fellow, a veteran peace officer replied:

"Sure, I know him: he's an exerter from the army—a pugilist from justice going under a consumed name."

At Ranger during the oil boom, there were thirty killings in the space of a few months, and not a man so much as sent to the penitentiary.

One night two no-account fellows had a row in a cheap dance hall and one stuck a knife in the other and walked slowly around him. They placed the assailant in the Ranger jail but it was ten miles to Eastland, the county seat, and the road was congested and muddy, so the county authorities neglected to file a charge.

The man's lawyer went to City Judge Flewellen and said:

"My client is being deprived of his liberty in violation of the Constitutional guarantees. He's willing to pay a nominal fine to the city if you'll turn him out."

Flewellen investigated and found that the deceased had provoked the difficulty but the judge felt that the city was entitled to something as the prisoner had been wearing out the Ranger jail for three days. So the judge decided to set a precedent and punish a man for murder in Eastland County.

He had the prisoner brought in and then, in stern tones, Judge Flewellen said:

"You can't come into our peaceful little community and strike down one of our leading citizens and not expect to feel the weighty hand of the law."

"I fine you seventy-five dollars for murder!

"I advise you to catch the next train out of town and let your first stop be Shanghai, China.

"I want this to be a lesson to you. If you ever kill another one of our citizens, I'll give you the full limit of the law—two hundred dollars and costs. Call the next case!"

* * * * * * *

A few years ago (it is related) Judge Flewellen was appearing as attorney for the plaintiff in a lawsuit before a rural Justice of the Peace in Eastland County and closed his argument in these words:

"Your Honor, you should decide this case in favor of the plaintiff. In fact, Your Honor, you should decide all cases in favor of the plaintiff—because, if it were not for plaintiffs, you would have no lawsuits and, therefore, no fees.

"Did Your Honor ever hear of a defendant filing a lawsuit?"

The judge stroked his long whiskers a moment, reflectively, and then said:

"No, I never did—I find in favor of the plaintiff!"

Ben Thompson, renowned wielder of the six-gun, became angry at the State Cattle-raisers Association— (one version is that it was because his friend, the Congressman from the Austin district, was not invited to address the convention).

Anyway, while one of the convention banquets was in progress in a Capital City hotel, Thompson entered the dining hall and began shooting the plates in front of the diners. This created a general stampede.

Afterward, one of the cattlemen was telling about it:

"You claim Ben Thompson is tough, huh? He got mad at our association but did he jump on the whole convention? No, sir-ee. He waited until he caught 50 or 60 of us off to ourselves."

* * * * * * *

Raymond Allred, brother of the former governor, used to be prosecuting attorney in a thinly-settled Panhandle district. A Chicago gangster strayed into the region and was arrested. After he had been questioned by the sheriff and his deputies, it was decided that he probably was ready to make a statement so he was locked in the room with the short, chunky and youthful prosecutor.

"Send for the D. A." said the prisoner.

"What?" asked Allred.

"The D. A. The district attorney. Don't you understand English?" the thug asked, impatiently.

"Oh, I'm the district attorney," Allred replied.

The racketeer looked him over and drawled:

"Gawd A'mighty!"

The fugitive then explained:

"I went over to the South Side to muscle in on the alky racket and a coupla harness bulls threw me in the hoosegow and after my mouthpiece made my bond I decided I was hot and had better take it on the lam."

Of course, that made everything clear.

* * * * * * *

One of the most venerable of all the West Texas stories:

Four men, one of them being one-eyed, were playing poker in a saloon in the old days. Suddenly, one of the men yanked out a pistol and said:

"I ain't callin' no names; but the next feller I see dealin' from the bottom of the deck, I'm gonna shoot his other eye out!"

34

A widow, to save her four children from starving took a cow that belonged to a ranchman.

She was indicted for cow-theft—a grave offense.

The woman told her sad story and the jury of chivalric sons of the West returned a verdict:

"We, the jury, find that the defendant stole the cow but she stole it in self-defense."

* * * * * *

A "bad man," in a bad mood from bad liquor, entered a saloon, flourished a pair of pistols and bellowed:

"I'll give every blankety-blank so and so thirty seconds to clear out."

There was a stampede for the exists. One little man in the corner, however, continued to drink his beer calmly.

"Did you hear what I said?" the two-gun man shouted.

"Yes," the other replied, "and there sure was a lot of them, wasn't there?"

* * * * * *

The justice of the peace at Mansker Lake (a small community, no longer in existence, in Eastland County) tried a man for carrying a pistol and, because the defendant had created a disturbance at a dance, the jurist decided to make an example of him and sentenced him to two years in the penitentiary!

The constable started out in a buggy with the prisoner for Huntsville. They stopped in Stephenville for lunch and a lawyer who knew the officer said:

"What are you taking him to Huntsville for?"

"Two years."

"I mean for what offense?"

"Carrying a pistol."

"What! Who imposed that sentence?" Informed that it was the Mansker Lake justice of the peace, the attorney said:

"Carrying a pistol is only a misdemeanor, which means that a fine or, at most, a jail sentence is the penalty. But if it carried a penitentiary sentence, the case would have to be tried before a district judge at the courthouse in Eastland—the justice of the peace wouldn't have jurisdiction."

So the constable turned the prisoner loose and returned to report to the magistrate:

"That lawyer feller said you didn't have jurisdiction."

"Jurisdiction, h——! It happened right here in my precinct, didn't it? I'm a-gonna resign."

35

A little boy, attending Sunday School for the first time, heard the story of the crucifixion. Much impressed, he told his parents about it later and concluded:

"It sure was too bad that the Texas Rangers weren't there."

*　　*　　*　　*　　*　　*　　*

The horse-thief was about to be hanged but a lawyer who was a newcomer in the frontier community insisted there ought to be a trial. So a judge was appointed, jury chosen, evidence heard and then the jury retired to the only vacant store-room in town to deliberate. After an hour, someone knocked on the door and asked:

"Ain't you fellows about ready to report? We need that room to put the corpse in."

*　　*　　*　　*　　*　　*

The town "bad man" attended a revival and was so deeply touched by the revivalist's appeal that he went to the mourner's bench.

"Confess your misdeeds," the preacher urged—but the man shook his head.

"The Lord will forgive you," the evangelist persisted.

"Yes," the sinner answered, "but the Lord ain't on the grand jury."

*　　*　　*　　*　　*　　*　　*

In the old days, a condemned man was put to death by hanging and the execution was held in the county seat where he had been convicted. On one occasion, a murderer was led to the scaffold but the sheriff, looking at his watch, noticed that it was a quarter of 12, so he said:

"John, you have 15 minutes more of life. Don't you want to deliver some kind of message of warning to all these people who are gathered here?"

The prisoner said:

"I reckon not; I'll just smoke my pipe during these last 15 minutes."

There was a little stir in the crowd and up the steps came a perpetual candidate for office.

"If the condemned man doesn't want to say anything, I would like to utilize the quarter of an hour in a discussion of the tariff," the professional windjammer began.

"Hold on!" the prisoner commanded. "Mr. Sheriff, if that feller is gonna make a speech, just hang me right now."

Bill was going to be electrocuted in a few days.

His soon-to-be widow visited him in Death Row at Huntsville and asked:

"Will it be all right for me and the children to attend the electrocution?"

The condemned man said:

"I'd rather you wouldn't."

His wife retorted:

"That's just like you, Bill—never wantin' us to have no pleasure in life."

*　　*　　*　　*　　*　　*　　*

"They Never Knew, for Sure" is the title of the masterpiece of Gene Cooper, raconteur de luxe:

He was often in front of a little restaurant in Round Rock that goes under the name you know that one place in Round Rock would be called—the Sam Bass Cafe. For it was in that town, some twenty miles north of the State capital, that Sam Bass, Texas' most notorious desperado of the horseback and six-shooter days, was not quick enough on the draw. That was in the early summer of 1878. It is still the talk of the town.

A first visitor to Round Rock was bound to ask, "Who killed Sam Bass?" and the old man was always immediate narrator.

"Why, they never knew," he would say, twirling a deft finger through the trailing sweep of a mustache that must have been the pattern for the racing bicycle handlebar, "for sure, that is, they never knew.

"And I reckon there's no use you askin any further for, if anybody knew, I'd know."

Histories of frontier days agree pretty well that the outlaw was mortally wounded during a running gun-fight in the streets, with townspeople and Texas Rangers taking part. Here, though, was a somewhat different account.

"Well do I recollect," the old man would say, "yes, I recall that day as if it was only yesterday—though at the time I was just a little tyke.

"Seven years old, I reckon I was, a-goin' on eight. I recollect that, because Pa had given me a new saddle for my seventh birthday. Not new, neither, but new to me, and in good leather and one I could grow to.

"That day I was home alone.

"There was a big commotion down in Round Rock—shootin', blowin' of cowhorns, and somebody rung the fire-bell.

"Of course," his hand passing across to shape the drift of the other half of the rich growth of his mustache, "kidlike, I had to find out what was a-goin' on. Home alone, because Pa was a-helpin' the Travises with the wheat harvest and Ma, suddenlike, had been called to the Browns, the tenants on the quarter-section across Brushy Creek, and she was still over there midwifin'.

"So I saddled my pony, Davy, and I took down Pa's gun from above the mantel—a .45-.70 brass lock, rimfire English sportin' rifle, the only one of its caliber in this Congressional deestrick. And I rid down toward Round Rock.

"Half way down the hill, I met two men at a long lope the other way, ridin' up the bluff across Brushy, and I hollered at 'em, 'Halloo, there,' but they didn't answer. They just rid on faster and one of 'em swung off down beyond a knoll. The other one wheeled and faced my way but he didn't 'halloo' back.

"So then, I offed my pony, and across the pommel of my saddle, the new saddle Pa give me for my seventh birthday—not new, neither, but new to me—with Pa's rifle, the .45-.70 brass lock, rimfire English sporter, the only one of that caliber in these parts, and I had a coupla clips at him.

"His horse bolted out of sight in a draw and I rid on down to Round Rock.

"Sure enough, there was a commotion. It was Sam Bass and his bandit gang caused it all. Tried to rob the bank. Posses was gettin' together right then. One of the band was killed and they was a-goin' after Sam Bass and another, who had rid off. Up Brushy Creek, some said.

"Well, sir, next day they found Sam Bass. Dead. In a little ravine just across Brushy Creek.

"Shot twice, he was; twice, through the heart; with bullets, they could tell, from a .45-.70.

"But," the old man said with a final flourish to the twist of his mustache, *"quien sabe? who knows?"*

And they never knew, not for sure, who killed Sam Bass.

A TOUCH OF "COLOR"

A new preacher had just announced his text when he was hit squarely in the mouth by a ripe tomato.

He wiped the debris away and then said:

"Bredern an' sistern, fer de next thutty minutes I'se gwine to preach a powerful Gospel sermon and, ef you'll stick aroun', after dat, youse gwine to see de d——edest fight you ever seen!"

*   *   *   *   *   *   *

A funeral sermon was in progress in a colored church when the "corpse" rose up in the casket.

There was a wild rush and several mourners were badly injured. At the official investigation, a colored woman objected to telling what she had heard the minister say as he dashed through the throng. But the justice of the peace ruled she would have to repeat the words, so she testified:

"De Reveren' say, D—— a architect who'd build a church wid only one door!"

Pastor Jones devoted his entire sermon to theft.
"Stealin' watermelons is wrong," he shouted.
"Amen," said Uncle Zeke.
"Stealin' chickens is wrong," the exhorter declared.
"Amen," again said Uncle Zeke.
"Stealin' ducks an' geese is wrong."
"Amen," once more chimed Uncle Zeke.
After the sermon, he confided to a friend:
"Ef he'd a-mentioned turkeys, he'd a-had me."

* * * * * * *

Texas definition of "dice":
Galloping dominoes.

* * * * * * *

A negro, wearing a flashing gem about the size of a locomotive headlight, was asked by an awestruck friend:
"Is dat diamond genuine?"
To which the proud possessor replied:
"Ef it ain't, I done been beat out of a dollah and a half."

* * * * * * *

A negro was telling a friend about the sermon he had heard that morning.
"De preacher show did preach a fine one; he spoke for nigh about two hours."
The friend asked:
"What was his subject?"
"He nevah did say," was the answer.

* * * * * * *

Along in the 1920's, the "Invisible Empire" was flourishing and—not saying there was any connection—a wave of whippings and tar-and-feather parties swept over the State.
Two negroes were talking on the street one day and one of them asked:
"Joe, whut would you do ef you got a letter from de Ku Klux?"
The other answered:
"I'd finish readin' it on de train."

* * * * * * *

Said a shine-boy in Eastland:
"I'se a-chewin' up dictionaries and a-spittin' out vocabularies."

40

A negro ran past his house with a razor-wielder in pursuit. Standing in the doorway, the wife of the fleeing darkey asked: "Wherefore is you runnin'?"

The pair circled the block and as they sped by, the woman repeated her question. Her husband gasped:

"Don't stand there askin' fool questions; have dat gate open de next time I come by!"

*   *   *   *   *   *   *

A negro parson was discoursing on the misdeeds of his race. He had spoken of intoxication, shooting craps and had reached the subject of stealing.

"It ain't right to go aroun' robbin' watermelons patches," he said.

At this statement, a brother in the third row snapped his fingers.

"Bruddah Brown, wherefore does you snap yoah fingers?" the minister asked.

"I jest remembahed where I left my pocket-knife," he answered.

*   *   *   *   *   *   *

The new minister was invited home by Deacon Jones for Sunday dinner.

The pastor praised the meal, particularly the fried chicken and inquired:

"Deacon, where did you get de chicken?"

To which his host countered:

"Bruddah, you is from de Nawth, ain't you?"

"Yes—but why?"

"Because no gem'man in de South evah asks annuddah where he gits his chickens."

*   *   *   *   *   *   *

And imagine the embarrassment of the colored parson who found one of his church members in Judge Smith's hen-roost one night!

*   *   *   *   *   *   *

A white man gave a negro a pint of whisky. A week later, they met and the donor asked how the whisky was.

"Jest right," said the darkey.

"What do you mean?" inquired the white man.

"Ef it had been bettah, you'd a-kept it; and ef it had been worser, I couldn't a-drunk it, so it was jest right."

41

Uncle Rastus didn't want to go past the cemetery after dark. "I ain't afraid o' dead folks," he explained, "but when people gets through walkin' and talkin', I'se through wid them."

* * * * * * *

Illustrating the potency of prayer, a colored deacon said:
"Ef I prays for chicken, sometimes I gets it an' sometimes I don't; but ef I prays the Lawd to send me aftah a chicken, I always gets one."

* * * * * * *

A colored woman called out to her daughter:
"Tell that niggah to quit huggin' an' kissin' you."
To which the girl replied:
"Tell him yoahsef; he's a puffick stranger to me."

* * * * * * *

George had "beat up" on a negro woman and he was explaining to the judge how it happened:
"It was like this. That niggah gal didn't have no teeth and she promised to marry me ef I got her a set. So I bought her a set o' teeth for forty dollahs. Then she th'owed me ovah and took up wid anuddah niggah.
"Yistiddy, I seen 'em togedder and she grinned at me—grinned at me wid my own teeth, jedge, an' I slapped h—— outta her."

* * * * * * *

Congressman Fritz Lanham of Fort Worth tells this story:
A colored preacher was delivering a fervent sermon. "We must quit dis back-bitin'," he intoned and two "sisters" on the front row exclaimed, "Amen, bruddah, amen."
"We must quit dis gossipin'," he continued.
"Amen, bruddah, amen," they chorused.
"And we must quit dis dippin' snuff," he shouted.
The two "sisters" exchanged glances and one of them muttered, "He's done quit preachin' an' gone to meddlin' now."

* * * * * * *

One of Senator Tom Connally's favorite stories:
Two negroes were standing in front of a bank in Marlin and one slowly read, "Capital and surplus, $1,000,000" and then he asked his friend, "Sam, ef you had a million dollahs, whut would you do wid it?"
Sam thought a moment and then replied, "I'd pay it on mah debts jest as far as it would go."

"FRIENDS AND FELLOW CITIZENS"

Texas once was represented in the national legislative halls by a man whose friends described him as "progressive" but whose enemies called him "ultra-radical."

It was an enemy who said that the lawmaker once addressed a Communist convention. There was absolutely no applause at the close of the speech and the orator asked the chairman why.

"Well," the chairman replied, "even we Communists believe in some form of government!"

* * * * * * *

Ed Kilman, while Capitol correspondent for the Houston Post, thus described a debate between two freshmen members of the House, each of whom was hypnotized by his own loud voice:

"Representative Blank and Representative Doakes engaged in intellectual combat today. Both were unarmed."

43

Clever phrasing was achieved by Cullen Thomas, candidate for United States Senator, who declared at a time when the Ku Klux Klan was powerful, back in the '20's:

"I am opposed to any clandestine organization," emphasizing the first syllable of the next-to-the last word.

* * * * * * *

Ed Clark, former Secretary of State, says that after he had expressed some view very firmly in his boyhood days, his wise grandfather would tell a story. Even though young Ed would protest that he had heard the story many times before, the old gentleman would insist on telling it again. Apparently he thought that the lad had missed the significance of the incident:

"I used to have (the grandfather would say) an Indian tenant on one of my farms. One day when I was visiting his place, an owl hooted and the Indian said, 'Um—will rain.' A week later, when I returned, there had been no break in the extremely dry weather and I reminded the Indian of his prediction. He replied:

" 'Um—young owl; d—— fool!' "

* * * * * * *

Election of W. Lee O'Daniel, the Hillbilly biscuit radio salesman as governor, caused one writer to announce that he was going to write a history of Texas to be entitled, "Under Six Flags—and a Flour Sack."

* * * * * * *

The vice chairman of the Senate committee on education said:

"I am opposed to this bill.

"In the first place, it ain't wrote right.

"And, in the second place, it ought to incarcerate some provision giving recognition to those in the more obscene walks of life."

* * * * * * *

Texans like their politics rough and ready, as you have seen by now.

The first time a prohibition plank was proposed at a State Democratic convention, a lusty-lunged speaker bellowed:

"Mr. Chairman, I move that we lay the resolution on the table and the author of the resolution under the table."

Which—more or less—was done.

A committee of the House was considering a bill for an appropriation when one member asked:

"Where will we get the money?"

A new member spoke up immediately:

"Oh, are we going to get some money?"

*   *   *   *   *   *   *

When Pat Neff ran for governor on a "bone-dry" platform, he declared he was going to make Texas so dry "that a man will have to prime himself before he can spit."

*   *   *   *   *   *   *

When Governor Neff visited the penitentiary, an elderly negro approached him and said, "Guv'nor, I wants clemency." Neff asked, "What are you serving?" The prisoner replied, "I'se servin' two life sentences." The Governor said, "In that case, I'll cut your punishment in two; you'll have to serve only one life sentence." The darkey answered, "Thank you, Guv'nor, thank you."

*   *   *   *   *   *   *

The occasion was the State reunion of Confederate veterans, some years back.

Everyone present had worn the "gray" or was the son or the daughter of a follower of the Lost Cause. The "Stars and Bars" adorned the speakers' stand. On one side was a picture of Robert E. Lee and, on the other side, a picture of Jefferson Davis. The band played "Dixie" and then the orator of the day was introduced—a high State official.

He reached the climax of his oration in these words:

"Fellow citizens, I am willing to bare my breast to the slings and arrows of those who will disagree with me but I want to tell you that in my candid judgment the Confederacy was right!"

*   *   *   *   *   *   *

"I'm a candidate for county judge," said an aspirant for office.

"Yes," the voter said, "I heard a bunch of the boys laughing about it down at the barber shop this morning."

*   *   *   *   *   *   *

A disgusted opponent of "Farmer Jim" and "Ma" Ferguson:

"In some of those East Texas counties, there's only one name that you could put on the ballot that would get more votes than Ferguson—Levi Garrett" (snuff manufacturer).

45

Dallas County has eight district judges, one of whom is Sarah Hughes, only woman jurist in the State. Someone referred to the group as Snow White and the Seven Dwarfs.

* * * * * * *

Of a certain orator, it was said:
"Invincible in time of peace, invisible in time of war."

* * * * * * *

Texas had a Governor quite a few years ago who had no book-larnin'. He thought "grammar" was father's mother. Every time he made a speech, he left the English language bleeding at every pore.

The question was asked, "What is the difference between Julius Caesar and the Governor?"

The answer was, "Caesar came, he saw, he conquered—the Governor come, he seed, he taken."

* * * * * * *

This same statesman was urging economy with public funds:
"They're wastin' yore tax money a-teachin' Latin an' Greek in the schools. That ain't necessary. English was good enough for Jesus Christ, wasn't it?"

* * * * * * *

This is a specimen of campaign oratory in the backwoods of Texas:

"They would have you believe that Colonel Splutterfuss is a prohibitionist and never took a drink in his life. But they don't deny he belongs to the Houston Club.

"Suppose you walked into the Houston Club. What could you order? Let's consult this menu (holding up a copy of a menu of the Houston Club).

"First, there's a fruit cocktail. You all know what a cocktail is. There a Manhattan cocktail and a Martini cocktail, and they even squirt a little fruit juice in one and call it a fruit cocktail.

"Next, there is consomme, a French wine.

"Then there is a filet mignon, a Russian drink four times stronger than vodka.

"And the last thing is a demi-tasse, which has sent many a strong man reeling into an untimely grave.

"Not a pork chop or a single item of food on the list!

"Don't take my word for it. Step right up here and see for yourself."

A wit remarked, "A cyclone is a vacuum surrounded by wind—and so is the Rev. John Blank," referring to a political preacher.

* * * * * * *

When Mrs. Miriam A. Ferguson was governor of Texas, her husband was generally credited with having considerable to do with acts and policies of the administration.

At any rate, "Farmer Jim," a former governor himself, had promised the voters that, when his wife was elected, he would "carry in the wood and water."

Mrs. Ferguson made liberal use of executive clemency.

One day (so a story goes) she was in an elevator in the Capitol when a man stepped on her foot.

"Pardon me," he said.

She replied, "You'll have to see Jim."

* * * * * * *

A speaker at a farmer's picnic:

"You have only three friends in the world—God Almighty, Montgomery Ward and Jim Ferguson."

* * * * * * *

Every year, the little town of Burkett in Central West Texas has a big picnic and the principal speaker is some noted political figure. One year, they were able to obtain the promise of probably the ablest stump-speaker in Texas to make an address, who —let us say—was named Joe Zilch; so the committee decided that the town would close for the occasion.

However, while the chairman was introducing the famous politician, who had a rather spotted record, one of the committeemen happened to notice that a little shop, owned by a citizen of foreign birth, was still open, so he dropped off the platform, hurried over and said:

"Ikey, why aren't you closed?"

The merchant asked:

"For why should I close?"

"Joe Zilch is in town."

"Vell," responded Ikey, "he von't hold me up in broad open daylight, vill he?"

* * * * * * *

Said a candidate for county office in West Texas:

"I ain't a-runnin' on my opponent's demerits—I'm a-runnin' on my own demerits."

He was elected, too.

A Texas "would-be" politician was running for sheriff in one of our many sparsely populated counties, and after he had traveled all over the county many times, working hard to win the office, election day finally came and he learned the next day that he had received the sum total of only one vote.

He stayed at home that day, nursing his disappointment, but the next day decided to go to town. He was walking down the street when he met his preacher. His preacher told him, "Wal, Henry, I remembered Sattidy what a faithful church-goer you've been for years, so I cast that one vote for you." The man replied, "Thanks, preacher."

As he went on around the town square, he met his butcher, who remarked, "Well, Henry, I remembered Sattidy what a good customer of mine you've been, so I cast that one vote fer ye." The disappointed man thanked him and walked on. The same story was told him by every friend and acquaintance he had in the county.

Finally, late that afternoon, he walked very dejectedly into his home and was met by his wife, who asked him why he was looking so glum. He replied, "Honey, we're leaving this town and this county. I've always loved these people up till now, but I don't anymore. These people here are the biggest liars I ever saw. I cast that one vote for myself!"

* * * * * * *

A West Texas candidate for county office had difficulty in remembering names as he went about handshaking at the picnics. But he told this story and was elected:

I once knew a preacher, and a mighty good one, too, but he couldn't remember folks' names. So when he had to deliver an address, if he had to use some names, he wrote them on a small piece of paper, pinned the paper on the inside of his tie and then would glance down at the notations from time to time.

On this particular occasion, he was called upon to deliver a funeral sermon which he did, somewhat in this fashion:

"Brethren and sisters, we are assembled to pay the last tribute of respect to our dearly-beloved friend (glancing down at the note inside his tie) John Jones. Well do I remember back in (pause) 1897 when he came into our midst and soon afterward married (pause) Mary Smith. But after many years spent as a noble citizen, husband and father, our good brother rests in the arms of his blessed Savior (pausing to glance at the note) Jesus Christ."

48

Politics in West Texas is virile. Here is a story (expurgated) that was used in a heated campaign:

A negro was brought before the judge for pounding another negro into insensibility. The defendant explained:

"Jedge, it wuz thissa way. He called me a yellow, kinky-headed so-and-so and I beat h—— outta him. Wouldn't you do the same thing if somebody called you that?"

Smiling, the judge said:

"No, Sam, because you see I'm not a yellow, kinky-headed so-and-so."

"Well, jedge, suppose somebody called you the kinda so-and-so what you is?"

* * * * * * *

Senator Joe Bailey is credited with the statement, "The greatest favor the Almighty bestowed on Texas was placing Oklahoma between Texas and Kansas."

* * * * * * *

A Texas Senator called a rather pompous judge over the telephone and, by way of a jest, told him that a bill had been introduced in the House to abolish his position. The jurist, his voice quivering with indignation, demanded:

"Who is backing this nefarious measure, Senator?"

"If you insist, it becames my painful duty to tell you that Representative Smithers of your home county is one of the authors," the Senator replied.

"Yes, that loathsome wolf in the grass; that snake in sheep's clothing. Who else is behind this infernal outrage?"

"I regret to inform you that Representative Zander also of your home county is co-author of the bill," the Senator answered.

"Yes, that contemptible scoundrel. He pretends to be my friend but he never had me fooled for a minute. He fawns upon me and all the time he is trying to stab me to the heart with a poisoned dagger."

Figuring that the matter had gone far enough, the Senator said:

"Judge, I was really only joking. The bill introduced doesn't apply to your court at all and neither of the men I named had anything to do with the bill."

There was a pause and then the judge responded:

"Senator, I resent your conduct on this occasion. You have caused me to say some very harsh things about two dearly beloved friends of mine."

A classic is the characterization that one eminent Texas politician bestowed upon another:

"When God Almighty created Bill Spivus, He wrote 'Without recourse on Me' across his face."

* * * * * * *

The need in politics is more frankness and courage such as characterized one spellbinder:

"My friends, I will make this assertion: I will defend it on every stump and I will risk my entire political future upon it— that Texas, my fellow countrymen, is the biggest State in the American Union!"

* * * * * * *

In Austin, the capital city, there are two newspapers, the Morning American and the Evening Statesman. Of each new legislator, it is related that as he alighted from the train there for the first time, he was greeted by a newsboy with:

"Evening Statesman."

"Fine, how are you?" the beaming lawmaker replied.

* * * * * * *

Hick Halcomb was a picturesque figure. He made a race for the Legislature when repeal of the prohibition amendment was under consideration, it is related. Sentiment was sharply divided in the district and so, when someone called out from the audience, "How about liquor?" Halcomb pretended not to hear him. But when the query was repeated, Halcomb paused impressively, then said:

"My friend, I am glad you asked me that. I am always happy to state my views in frank, clear-cut fashion on any issue.

"I want to say that you can not make a people good by law; you can not legislate morals into a man." (Cheers from the "wets").

"But, on the other hand, you can repeal all the prohibition laws in Christendom but you can not repeal the harmful effects of alcohol upon the human body, mind and soul." (Cheers from the "drys").

"And now, my friends, I pass on to the tariff question."

* * * * * * *

A candidate for prosecuting attorney in West Texas promised:

"If I'm elected, I'll make the bootleggers think that the mouth of h—— is just thirty feet from the courthouse door."

Hick not only was a master in the field of anecdote but also in the rapier thrust of repartee.

If the name of someone he especially disliked came into the conversation, Halcomb would exclaim, "Why did you mention that fellow? I wouldn't have thought of him for half a dollar."

Another expression of his concerning a "dumb cluck" who was distasteful was, "He's studying to be a half-wit—but I don't think he'll make it."

And when a friend scored on Hick, he was likely to say something like:

"I never forget a face but, Joe, I'll be glad to make an exception in your case."

* * * * * * *

A local option election was being held in a county inhabited by sturdy Germans, who loved the foaming brew.

The teller called out:

"Vet, vet, vet, vet"—then frowning he said: "Dry-y-y." Then he continued:

"Vet, vet, vet, vet." His brow clouded as he exclaimed:

"The son-of-a-gun! He voted twice!"

* * * * * * *

An aspirant for the governorship said that an opponent—who had made a great noise on anti-trust activities while attorney general—reminded him of a dog he used to own.

"We'd build a fire out on the prairie and have supper and then that dog would take out after a wolf," the candidate related, "and old Blucher knew just how fast to run not to catch up with that wolf."

* * * * * * *

Another candidate, talking about the same opponent, said he, too, was reminded of a dog, whose owner—a darkey—claimed he could tell from Tige's bark just what he was after. A white man bet $5 he couldn't.

So old Tige was sent on a circle and pretty soon, he barked, off in the woods.

"What's he after?" the white man asked.

"I nevah heerd 'im bark jest like dat befo'; I wants to hear 'im again," replied the owner.

In a little while, Tige barked again.

"All right, tell me what he's after?" the other demanded.

"I ain't shore but I believes somethins' after Tige," the negro replied.

51

Some years ago, floodlights were installed and the Capitol was nightly bathed in light. A legislator explained:

"We did that to make sure that the governor wouldn't steal the dome."

* * * * * * *

It used to be the custom, when a man was sentenced to death in Texas, to hang him at the county seat where he had been convicted. Such hangings were spectacles which sometimes attracted thousands of persons.

A bill was passed some years ago to have all executions at the penitentiary in Huntsville and to substitute the electric chair for hanging.

Former State Senator Lloyd Price declares that when the bill was being debated, one legislator opposed both features somewhat in this language:

"Mr. Speaker, there has been an alarming movement-t-t of people from the country and small towns into our great cities. One of the causes of this unhealthy concentration of population has been the lack of amusement-t-t in the small towns.

"This bill would aggravate an already bad condition by taking away one of the few remaining amusement-t-t-s available to our rural population.

"And as for the electric chair, I want to say, Mr. Speaker, that hanging was good enough for my dear, old father, and it's good enough for me!"

* * * * * * *

The favorite Texas story of J. Frank Dobie, widely-known historian and folklorist, is one about Sam Houston.

They gave a big outdoor dinner in Houston's honor: they put the big pot in the little one, fried the skillet and threw away the handle, as the saying goes. Old Sam was surrounded by a crowd and he ate and talked and talked and ate; his eating didn't interfere with his talking, and his talking didn't interfere with his eating.

Somebody handed him a bowl of hot rice pudding, than which nothing can be hotter. In the middle of a sentence, Houston lifted a big spoonful to his generous-sized mouth—and, the next instant, spat out the fiery mouthful, exclaiming:

"Many a durn fool woulda swallowed that!"

When James V. Allred—Attorney General, Governor and Federal Judge—was making his first race for chief executive of the State, he criticized the platform of his opponent for its vagueness.

Allred said, "My opponent reminds me of Christopher Columbus. When Columbus set out, he didn't know where he was going, when he got there, he didn't know where he was; and when he got back, he couldn't tell folks where in thunder he'd been."

Continuing, Allred said that he called to mind an inscription on a tomb in a country churchyard:

> "Good friend, pause, as you pass by;
> As you now are, so once was I;
> As I now am, you soon shall be:
> Prepare for death and follow me."

But (the candidate went on) one day a wag read the epitaph and then added these lines in pencil:

> "Wherever you are, I wish you well;
> Whether up in heaven or down in hell;
> But to follow you, I'm not content—
> Until I know which way you went."

* * * * * * *

Once upon a time there was a member of the legislature who liked to make speeches, which he did, loud and often. One day, a bill was coming up which he strongly favored and he sent up his name to speak. Word came back that he would be given three minutes. He went up to the presiding officer's stand and demanded:

"Why can't I have more time?"

"Because there's only 30 minutes to the side and nine others want to speak for the bill."

The representative reflected a moment, then asked:

"How many are down to speak on the other side?"

"Only two."

"Then put me down to speak against the bill—I'll get more time that way."

Ernest Cox is past commander of the American Legion of Texas. He is known to thousands as Ozro Cox because of a speech of his which went like this:

"I'm from Ozro.

"Ozro, at the time I was born there, was a little village consisting of a general merchandise store, blacksmith shop, cotton gin, schoolhouse and cemetery.

"It was right in the middle of that black waxy land belt, the kind of soil that will certainly stick with you in wet weather if you have the intestinal fortitude to stick with it in dry weather.

"It's located three miles from Griffith's Switch, three and a half miles from Stringtown, four from Auburn, five from Maypearl, six from Mountain Peak, six and a half from Boz and eight from Bethel.

"It is on the Meridian Highway just before you come to Bono, Nemo, Rainbow, Fort Spunkey and Baughhauffer Mill.

"My old Uncle John had always been a politician so it was just natural that when Bill, a son of his and of course a cousin of mine, got old enough to run for office, he made a determined campaign for constable and got the socks licked off of him.

"But that didn't faze him a bit. He threw his old hat back in the ring and got licked again. But when he announced a third time, one of the neighbors asked him to explain. All that Cousin Bill could say was:

" 'I'm naturally politicious.

" 'I come from a politicious family. Paw's a Democrat; Maw's a Republican; the baby's wet and the cow's dry and the dog's a durned old Socialist because he sets on his tail all day and howls and howls and howls'."

*　　*　　*　　*　　*　　*　　*

When United States Senator W. Lee O'Daniel was making his first, spectacularly-successful race for Governor of Texas, an opponent described him as a "flour salesman from Ohio."

Now it so happened that back in 1836 when Texas declared her independence from Mexico, citizens of Ohio purchased two cannon, which became famous as the "Twin Sisters," and sent them to the aid of the Texans.

O'Daniel's reply to his opponent was:

"He never heard of this gift from the people of Ohio and if you were to mention the Twin Sisters to him, he'd probably ask for their telephone number."

54

There was a Governor a long time ago who issued many pardons. Things were said about him—(unjust, no doubt). Once, so it was claimed, a man called on him to plead for a pardon for a son. The Governor kept calling the visitor's attention to a horse grazing in the yard and mentioned that he would be glad to sell the animal.

At last, the man broke in:

"But Governor, I don't want to buy a horse; I'm here to get a pardon for my boy. What good would a horse be to me, anyhow?"

The official softly replied:

"Your son could ride home from the penitentiary on him."

* * * * * * *

Hick Halcomb was editing a weekly paper up in the Panhandle and writing a "column" called "The World's Worst Hick," when he decided to run for the legislature. In announcing his candidacy, he declared that he was running for two reasons:

"First, because I want the $10 a day—it will be the most money I ever made in my life; and, second, because I want a free, ringside seat at the world's biggest show, the Texas legislature in session."

There was a flock of candidates for the place and they "joint debated" over the district. One of Hick's rivals eloquently erupted:

"Ladies and gentlemen, there's one man in this race whose position is indefensible. He says he's a-running for the $10 a day. I don't care whether the place pays $10 or $8 or $4 a day; it doesn't matter what the salary is—I'm a-running for the opportunity to be of service to my fellow man."

The irrepressible Hick retorted:

"My opponent reminds me of a boy in my native village who applied for a job in the bank. The president said, 'But we don't have an appropriation for another salary.' He said, 'That's all right; I'm willing to work for what I can pick up around the place'."

* * * * * * *

A county commissioner saw a farmer who had supported his opponent two years previously. The official shook hands and said, "Joe, I know you weren't for me last time; but I'm running again and I'd like to have your support." The farmer said, "Well, Commiissioner, I reckon I'll be fer you; I don't know that other so-and-so that's runnin' agin you."

GOLD THAT GUSHES— SOME- TIMES

An elderly farmer, made rich by a new gusher on his farm, bought himself a new car, a suit of clothes and a gold watch.

"Aren't you going to buy something for your wife?" a friend asked.

So he bought a new handle for the ax.

* * * * * * *

In the "grass-roots" field around Moran, oil is struck at such a shallow depth that wells are drilled with a carpenter's brace-and-bit (so they say) and notices are posted on the gates:

"Men with peg-legs, keep out!"

* * * * * * *

A farmer on whose land a test for oil was being drilled thought he ought to receive any information he desired. He asked a roughneck, "How deep are you?" and the answer was, "We're drilling in h—— right now."

The farmer complained to the superintendent, who rebuked the roughneck and wound up by saying, "You know good and well that we drilled through h—— three days ago."

A driller was explaining his finances to a friend:

"I make $300 a month. I pay twenty dollars for a room; thirty dollars for meals; fifteen dollars for clothes, and the rest of it I spend on the necessities of life."

* * * * * * *

Another driller put it this way:

"After I take out for food, clothes and rent I only have $60 left for the necessities of life and half the time they ain't hardly fitten to drink."

* * * * * * *

"Did you hear about Brown making $30,000 on a gold mine?"

"Yes, only it wasn't Brown, it was Jones; and it wasn't $30,000, it was $80,000; and it wasn't a gold mine, it was an oil well; and he didn't make it—he lost it!"

* * * * * * *

Ned Alvord, picturesque, old-time circus press-agent, remarked:

"They're building monuments to Sam Houston when all he ever done was to face Mexican bullets on the battle-field; I ate in the cafes of Longview during the oil boom!"

* * * * * * *

A minister in the East Texas oil field was praying:

"Oh, Lord, bless the pure and the humble."

A member of the flock broke in:

"Never mind the Pure and the Humble; bless the Dry Hole Oil Company—they need it."

* * * * * * *

There are ten times as many oil wells drilled in hotel lobbies as are ever actually drilled in the field.

A man haled before the city judge at Wichita Falls for vagrancy was asked:

"Don't you have any trade or profession?"

He answered, "Well, I was an oil man till some son-of-a-gun stole my map."

* * * * * * *

A stranger in a boom town (in, theoretically, prohibition days) asked:

"Where can a man get a drink of whiskey?"

Then one accosted said:

"See that building up yonder? Well, that's the postoffice. You can't get it there or at the Baptist Church."

Newly-rich from oil, a Ranger citizen decided to move to Dallas and he looked over several mansions with the idea of purchasing one. At last, the real estate man showed him a palace, priced at a quarter of a million dollars. The West Texan viewed the gold handles on the doors, the crystal chandeliers and the silken tapestries with mild interest. Suddenly his eye alighted on an object and he exclaimed "What's that?"

"It's a wall safe," the real estate man replied and opened it.

"That's just the place for my Woodman policy; I'll take the house," said the other.

* * * * * * *

Mud and oil are as much united as Daniel Webster's "Liberty and Union, now and forever, one and inseparable."

At Ranger, during the great boom, the main street was so muddy that there was a man with a horse and sled who charged folks a dime to haul them from one sidewalk to the other.

It is related that a pedestrian saw a new hat lying in the mud. When he picked it up, there came a shout from below:

"Gimme my hat back."

Looking down, the first man said:

"Is there somebody down there?"

"H——, yes," came from the depths.

"You must be in bad shape."

"No, I'm all right but this horse I'm ridin' ain't doin' so well."

* * * * * * *

Bootleggers in the old-time oil boom towns were so numerous that they wore badges so they wouldn't be trying to sell to each other.

* * * * * * *

In an oil boom town, crime is so rampant that you are liable to have the gold filling stolen from your mouth while you sleep. The canaries sing bass and the children bark back at the bulldogs.

* * * * * * *

A wealthy West Texas oil man who had been arrested several times for being intoxicated was sitting in a park one morning, after an eventful "night before," when a man walked up, identified himself as a detective and said he would like to have a dollar for flowers as "we are burying a policeman this afternoon."

The oil man said, "Here's $5; bury five of the blankety-blanks."

The Paul Bunyan of the Texas oil fields is Gib Morgan.

He was born in the eastern edge of Texas as the family was migrating. His earliest exploit occurred when he was only a few days old. Enormous mosquitoes attacked the camp and the baby was placed under a big wash-pot for protection and was given an axe with which to amuse himself.

The mosquitoes were not to be balked, however. One of them got back a hundred feet and launched himself like a torpedo at the kettle. So great was his momentum that his bill rammed through the iron as though it were only paper. Another followed his example and another.

Immediately after each had rammed into the kettle there came a "bing" from within.

When the father investigated, he found that as fast as a skeeter had thrust his bill through the pot, little Gib had bradded it with the axe!

* * * * * * *

When Morgan grew up, he became a driller.

Once he chose a lofty hill in West Texas as the location for a well. He had drilled to a depth of three thousand feet when along came a terrific wind and blew all the sand away, leaving three thousand feet of hole standing out in the open air.

Not at all dismayed, Gib sawed the hole into four-foot lengths, shipped them to Kansas and sold them to the farmers for ready-made post-holes.

* * * * * * *

One of Morgan's derricks was so high that the derrickman came down to the earth only twice a month—on paydays.

* * * * * * *

The mighty driller announced that he was going to sink the deepest well in the history of the world.

He built a derrick so tall that, halfway up, it was on hinges so the top would let down at night out of the way of the stars.

The crew, led by the tireless Morgan, drilled and drilled, and at last struck oil. One of the workers fell into the well and dropped clear through to China. He cabled back: "She's making 5,000 barrels a day at this end, too."

* * * * * * *

Morgan started one well that, only a few hundred feet down, hit a bed of alum and the hole shrank so much that it had to be abandoned.

Morgan was so considerate of his men that he once constructed a pipeline to bring them buttermilk.

And in one field, his derricks were so close together that it was necessary to "pipe" daylight to the ones in the center.

* * * * * * *

In the early days of oil, Morgan used black snakes for drilling cable.

And one of his first wells struck a white sand which yielded pure buttermilk.

* * * * * * *

Another derrick was so tall that, while Morgan and his men were building it, they moved to heaven and lived there till the derrick was finished.

* * * * * * *

Morgan was erecting a tank and dropped a hammer. The tank was so high that the hammer wore out two handles in falling to the ground.

* * * * * * *

When a big flow of oil was struck unexpectedly, Morgan sat on top of the hole but the oil increased and he was carried so high into the air that it took two days to build the derrick on up so he could be rescued.

On another occasion, when a boiler blew up, he jumped astride it and rode it back to earth.

* * * * * * *

Once Morgan was drilling in formation as hard as granite and he fitted up the heaviest drilling equipment ever known. The bit hit so hard that it lifted the whole fifty-acre tract thirty feet higher than the surrounding country.

* * * * * * *

Morgan was quite a marksman. He had an old-time rifle that he liked to use and he would shoot at a rubber target. The ball would hit the target and bounce back into the gun barrel and by that time he'd have a fresh charge of powder in place and would shoot again. One day, he was making a perfect score when he happened to hiccough and the ball missed the rifle barrel on the rebound and wounded him. It was just a flesh wound on the wrist but he gave up that style of shooting.

And Morgan used to kill deer at such a great distance that he used salted bullets—otherwise the meat would have spoiled before he could walk to it.

Once in a while, even as expert as Morgan was, he would have a misadventure.

He judged he was deep enough to drill into the oil sand, and so he started running casing. Well, sir, he put in an unbelievable amount of casing and still apparently the bottom hadn't been reached. So he decided to investigate, and he found that the drill had hit such a hard formation that the hole had been deflected and it had come out on the side of a mountain. He had run the pipe clear out of the hole and had laid two miles of pipe line in the valley.

* * * * * * *

Morgan had a wooden leg 30 feet long. (He was a very big man). Members of the crew wore out a wooden leg a week, climbing up it to bum him for cigarets.

* * * * * * *

Once when the drill was deflected, Morgan took a coring and found he had colored blankets, an Aztec calendar stone, a bottle of tequila and a couple of tourists—so he knew he had hit Mexico.

* * * * * * *

Once Morgan was drilling in India. The drill hit the root of a rubber tree and wouldn't quit bouncing, so the hole had to be abandoned.

This gave him an idea, however, and he perfected a rubber bit and when it was run in the hole and started bouncing, the crew didn't have to do anything till it was time to change bits.

* * * * * * *

Drilling in South America he hit a flow of rubber which drenched the derrick, then cooled. A worker, high up in the rig, lost his hold on the slippery timber and fell to the floor. He bounced for three days and nights before they shot him to keep him from starving to death.

* * * * * * *

Another well hit an even bigger flow of rubber which flooded the countryside in a solid sheet. The cook used the big doughnut cutter that he made doughnuts for Morgan with and punched out a lot of automobile tires. With what was left, Morgan made rubber boilers so that, no matter how high the temperature got, they would just stretch and stretch and not blow up.

Over one enormous derrick Morgan put a roof, so that when the great flow of oil came in, it wouldn't knock a hole in the sky.

This was the derrick that was so high that Morgan installed a telephone system with a 'phone for each member of the crew. As it took a man 14 days to climb to the top of the derrick, he had to hire 30 derrick men. There was a dog-house a day's journey apart for the men to rest in and there were always 14 men climbing up the derrick, another 14 men climbing down, one man on top and one off duty!

* * * * * * *

Morgan, mighty man of the oil fields, once took up ranching. He was displeased by the freight rates, and so he used oil field methods of transporatation; he built a pipe line from his ranch to the Fort Worth stockyards and pumped the cattle through the line. However, it was so big that the calves would get lost in the threads and would starve to death.

The pipe line also sprang a leak, and he lost 25 carloads of cattle before he found out about it and decided to abandon the line.

* * * * * * *

Probably the most ingenious of all Morgan's ideas, however had to do with dry holes. He decided that, being worthless over here, he might transplant them to Europe where they might prove to be oil wells.

Now he owned a big steer named Babe that was 42 or maybe only 41, pick-handled lengths between the eyes, so Morgan fastened a chain to Babe and the steer pulled up the dry holes with no trouble, except one which broke off in the middle.

Morgan loaded the dry holes on a ship but the rough voyage got them so warped that they were useless and had to be thrown away.

* * * * * * *

When a bit or other piece of equipment is lost in the bottom of a drilling well, it has to be "fished" out, often a slow and costly process. During the Ranger boom, a well was being drilled for a British syndicate and every day a cablegram was sent. One day, this message was dispatched: "Bit lost in hole." Next day, the report was: "Fishing" and the same report was given every day for a week. And then a reply from across the ocean was received: "If you don't quit fishing and get to work, we'll fire everyone of you."

Mining has its lure (along with the spell of oil) in Texas.

One prospector said: "I been a-huntin' for gold and silver for forty years and I ain't found nothin' but the prospects is good."

* * * * * * *

Concerning the legends of lost mines in the Chisos Mountains, one old-timer scornfully said:

"There ain't nothin' but legions in them Cheese Mountains."

* * * * * * *

A group of oil men were sitting around in the Spindletop field with nothin much to do when one of them suggested, "Let's make some lemonade."

So one of the oil men bought the lemons, another one provided the sugar, another one got the water and soon they had a large supply.

The first one began calling first to this and then to that passerby, inviting them over to have some of the lemonade. One of the others spoke up and said:

"Why are you getting so liberal? I furnish the sugar and the others put in the other things."

"Yes" rejoined the other, "but I promoted the idea."

That settled the discussion.

* * * * * * *

An oil man died and applied for admission to heaven. But Saint Peter said:

"There are too many oil men up here now; they're running all over the place prospecting and are liable to start building derricks in the golden streets at any moment."

The applicant replied:

"Let me in for a week and I'll promise to leave if I don't help the situation."

Saint Peter agreed and the newcomer went around to the others, one by one, and whispered:

"Did you hear they'd struck oil in h——?"

At the end of two days, every one of them had left and Saint Peter looked up the new arrival to thank him. But when he found the oil operator, Saint Peter was amazed to see that he had his suitcase packed and seemed about to depart.

"What does this mean?" the saint asked.

"I'm leaving for h——; there may be something to that report, after all."

MILD
AND
WOOLLY

A tenderfoot applied at a sheep ranch for food and lodging.

"Go out and drive the sheep into the corral," the rancher said.

So the Easterner set out. It was long after dark when he returned.

"I thought I never would get through," he explained. "I drove the sheep in all right but the lambs were h——."

"Lambs—we don't have any lambs this time o' year," the Texan said.

He went to the corral to investigate and found that the tenderfoot had rounded up nineteen jackrabbits.

* * * * * * *

A traveler through the semi-primitive "hill-country" just a few miles from the State Capitol reports seeing this sign on a gate:

"A few goats and a few votes for sale."

Regarding a cautious candidate for state office, the following is narrated:

Two newspaper correspondents made a wager as to whether a positive statement on any subject could be elicited from the candidate. The one who had bet in the affirmative was about to pay off after several failures to get the politician to commit himself on any matter.

But the scribe, out in San Angelo, saw a flock of sheep coming along the street. They had just been shorn as their close-clipped hides revealed, even to the uninitiate.

"Judge, those sheep are certainly sheared close," the correspondent ventured.

"They would appear to be on this side," was the reply.

The newspaperman gave up.

* * * * * * *

The new school marm asked a little boy at Ozona:

"If there were twelve sheep in a field and one jumped over the fence, how many would be left?"

The pupil said, "None."

The teacher said, "You don't know arithmetic."

"No, ma'am, but I know sheep," he replied.

* * * * * * *

A sheepman amazed his friends by his unerring accuracy in giving instantly the number of sheep in a flock.

Asked how many were in a flock passing by, he barely glanced, then said:

"Six hundred and seventeen."

The owner acknowledged that this was the correct total and inquired:

"How do you do it?"

"Oh, it's simple; I just count the number of legs, then divide by four."

* * * * * * *

When W. K. Gordon, "father of the Ranger oil field," was assembling the vast amount of leases his company held before beginning its exploration, he had to have a paper notarized, so he stopped at a farmhouse. He could see the farmer at work in the field and, to save a possibly useless walk, he asked the farmwife, "Is your husband a notary public?" She replied, "No, he's a Democrat."

"THE CITIES ARE FULL OF PRIDE"

★

"The gentleman from Odessa" is a term frequently heard in West Texas. This explanation was given by the inhabitant of a rival town:

"Have you ever wanted to call a man a so-and-so in mixed company? Well, a so-and-so would be a gentleman in Odessa."

So far from resenting the term, frequently a citizen from that town will smilingly introduce himself as "a gentleman from Odessa."

* * * * * * *

A motorist who was lost asked a farmer plowing in a field:
"How can I get to Austin?"
The farmer said:
"Go down this road two miles till you come to a bridge then turn right. No—on second thought, you'd better turn around and go back till you came to a schoolhouse and take the left turn. No—say, Mister, if I was goin' to Austin, I'll be durned if I'd start from here."

Olney used to have a hotel proprietor whose stationery proclaimed:

"Hot and cold water—hot in summer, cold in winter; all modern inconveniences; rates after I look 'em over."

* * * * * * *

A citizen was telling a stranger about a neighboring town:

"To give you an idea of what kind of a place it is, a man dropped dead in the door of the postoffice Thursday afternoon and the body was found Saturday morning by a Dallas traveling man who wanted to mail a letter."

* * * * * * *

That calls to mind the druggist in a small town back in prohibition days. He sold large quantities of jamaica ginger, a fiery alcoholic fluid. One day, a citizen noticed that one of the leading addicts, who spent most of the day in front of the drug store, was lying in the street, so the citizen entered the shop and said:

"Bill, your 'jake' sign has fallen down."

* * * * * * *

Incidentally, some pessimist has said:

There are three kinds of lies—lies, d—— lies and Chamber of Commerce statistics.

* * * * * * *

Then there was the Cisco citizen who said to the booster from Abilene:

"Your town ought to be a seaport and it can be, too."

Unsuspectingly, the Abilene man asked:

"But how?"

"Just lay a pipeline to the Gulf, and then if you can suck just half as hard as you can blow, you'll be a seaport in no time."

* * * * * * *

But Cisco is enterprising, too.

Rival editors declare that if a man on the "Sunshine Special" jumps off at Cisco, grabs a ham sandwich, jumps back on the train, continues on to California and—ten years later—he is killed by a truck or elected to Congress, the Cisco paper refers to him as "a former Ciscoan."

67

The remark that usually brings on the first blow when citizens of the two greatest rival cities in Texas meet:

Dallasite—Well, I'll admit that Fort Worth has one thing that Dallas doesn't have.

Fort Worthian—What's that?

Dallasite—A real city just thirty-three miles away.

* * * * * * *

Non-inflamable gas—known as helium—which is used in balloons is produced at Amarillo. An Eastener, visiting in Fort Worth, mentioned that his tour would include Amarillo.

"You want to be sure to see the helium plant in that city—it's the only one in the world," someone said.

"Thanks for telling me about that plant; I surely hope it's in bloom while I'm there," he replied.

* * * * * * *

The quiet little town of Georgetown, picturesquely situated beside two little rivers of green-and-white water that dashes over rocky beds, is the capital of Williamson County and the home of Southern University. As already stated, it is a calm place.

The following story, probably originated by some citizen of Taylor, a rival town in the same county, is told:

In early days, lawyers of Central Texas traveled from county seat to county seat during the court season. A visiting attorney was stricken while in Georgetown. The doctors told him he had only a few moments left.

"Well," he said, speaking each word with great effort, "I have never been in any place that I leave with less regret than Georgetown."

* * * * * * *

When a new cafe opened in Austin, someone remarked that he had heard the prices were high.

A former Senator said:

"I don't think so. I had breakfast there this morning and I got coffee, toast, two eggs, bacon and an overcoat, all for a quarter."

* * * * * * *

When Dallas built its first skyscraper, the citizens boasted that they had to keep the windows on the top story closed so as to keep the clouds out and that were going to take off the four top floors so Forth Worth could get some sunlight.

A wag said, "The girls bathe in Sweetwater and dress in Plainview and the men are all going to Seymour."

* * * * * * *

The first ice-plant in the United States was built in famous old Jefferson, at one time the second largest city in Texas. A member of a Hard Shell Baptist Church in East Texas returned from a visit to the metropolis one Summer and narrated the wonders he had seen.

"I actually saw 'em manufacturing ice," he declared.

So the other members were about to turn him out of the church for lying but one suggested that they ought to be fair and make an investigation first so he was appointed to go to Jefferson. He came back and reported:

"I know it's amazing but they actually were making ice and it the middle o' July and the temperature 98 in the shade."

So the church kicked them both out for lying.

* * * * * * *

In front of the dining room of the leading hotel in Gorman, there used to be a pair of scales. Each guest weighed before entering the dining room and weighed again on coming out and then paid four cents for each ounce gained.

One fellow, however, who knew about this had two brick bats in his pocket when he weighed in. He ate a huge dinner, slipped the brick bats under the table and when he weighed again, the hotel owed him 20 cents!

* * * * * * *

When towns are neighbors, there is always the temptation to say something humorously cutting about each other. A few samples (with correct names of the town omitted for quite obvious reasons) follow:

Possum Trot has just three things—morning, noon and night.

When the bank was held up a few years ago at Bunkville Corner, folks there thought it was done by Raymond Hamilton or Clyde Barrow; but, shucks, that town's living so far back in the past that it was the Dalton brothers or maybe Jesse James.

A Western Union boy going through Silo City last week was shot to death. The natives thought he was a Union spy.

* * * * * * *

The colored porter in the bus station at Eastland chants a rhyme:

"All aboard for Cisco, Hico, Waco—any place you wanna go."

Unique is the Bonehead Club of Dallas of which the late Dr. Joe J. Taylor, beloved editor of the Dallas News, was a leading spirit. The latest undertaking of the club is the construction of a twenty-one story office building. It is planned to build the upper twenty stories first and then, when a location is decided on, to construct the ground floor!

* * * * * * *

Am I right or Am-a-rillo?

* * * * * * *

Waxahachie and Ennis are rival cities in Ellis County—which, incidentally, sometimes leads the State in the production of cotton.

A suit on a note was going on before the justice of the peace in Waxahachie. The attorney for the defendant made several references to Shylock and the "Merchant of Venice."

The lawyer for the plaintiff said:

"Gentlemen of the jury, we've got just as good store-keepers right here in Waxahachie as you can find anywhere but my opponent keeps talking about some merchant over there at Ennis and I resent it!" He won the case.

* * * * * * *

In the Dallas union station, the traveler lugs his suitcases up steep stairs and then marches right down again on the other side for no apparent reason.

It is related that Harry K. Thaw (who killed Stanford White, builder of the original Madison Square Garden) once visited Dallas and, after going up, then down that useless set of stairs, Thaw exclaimed:

"My God, I killed the wrong architect!"

* * * * * * *

Best known town in Texas (invoked by crap-shooters throughout the world) :

"Eighter from Decatur, the county seat of Wise."

* * * * * * *

The courthouse at Stephenville has a large clock which, at night, is illuminated.

Late one night, a citizen rather unsteadily approached a mail box, dropped a penny in the slot, glanced up at the clock and exclaimed:

"Good heavens, I'm nine pounds over-weight!"

70

Former Congressman Guinn Williams of Decatur tells this one:

A merchant from a little town near Decatur was summoned for jury duty in federal court in Fort Worth.

"What is your name?" a lawyer asked.

"Solomon," was the response.

"Where are you from?"

"Paradise," said the juror.

"Where is that?" the astonished attorney inquired.

"Wise County," came the answer.

The lawyer said, musingly:

"Solomon, Paradise, Wise County—I don't believe we can use you."

* * * * * * *

Dublin (Texas, not Ireland), isn't so very large—about 4,000 people—but it is an important railroad point.

A traveling salesman said he had been on the road for thirty years, of which fourteen were spent in Dublin, waiting for trains.

* * * * * * *

Waco, then a city of perhaps 35,000, was proud possessor of one of the first skyscrapers in the State.

The inhabitants overlooked no chance to speak of it. If you asked the way to the postoffice, you would be told in this fashion:

"Do you see that tall building down yonder? Well, that's the Amicable Building. You go two blocks north from there and one east and there's the postoffice."

A traveling man who had to ask the location of several establishments at last grew weary of this formula so when someone inquired where he lived, he replied:

"Do you see that tall building down yonder? Well, that's the Amicable Building. You go four hundred and thirty-seven miles straight north and there's Oklahoma City—that's where I live."

* * * * * * *

Besides having the first skyscraper in Texas, Waco was—and is—famous as the home of Baylor University, the largest Baptist school in the world. Someone described Waco as "a tall building, entirely surrounded by Baptists."

71

If you visit Uvalde (which is famous for its honey), here's one story that you should refrain from telling because every citizen has heard it many, many times before:

A Uvalde citizen had a favorite cafe in San Antonio because there he could always get honey for his hot cakes. When he married, he and his bride went to San Antonio on their honeymoon. They visited the cafe and ordered hot cakes but when the waiter brought the cakes, he set a pitcher of syrup on the table.

The man looked up in surprise and asked:

"Where's my honey?"

"Oh, she don't work here no more," the waiter said.

* * * * * * *

A man who had just been shown to his room in a cheap hotel in Dallas telephoned excitedly to the clerk:

"Two bed-bugs are having a fight in the middle of the bed."

The clerk asked:

"How much did you pay for the room?"

"Seventy-five cents."

"What do you expect for seventy-five cents? Dempsey and Tunney?"

* * * * * * *

Folks familiar with the speed with which food disppears at the average boarding-house table will be interested in this incident, narrated concerning an institution of this character in the oil boom town of Odessa:

One of the boarders was chopping wood in the back yard when the dinner bell rang. He threw down his axe and started at a gallop but stumped his toe and fell.

Arising, he said, "Oh, h——, I wasn't hungry, anyway," picked up his axe and started chopping wood again.

* * * * * * *

Twisting as are the streets of San Antonio, the Texas city must yield the palm to Santa Fe, New Mexico, of which it has been said:

"The town was laid out by a drunk Indian on a blind mule in a sandstorm."

* * * * * * *

This description calls to mind the one about a painting which appeared to be simply a smear but the artist explained:

"This is a picture of a negro in a dark cellar at midnight looking for a black cat that isn't there."

Hog Town on Hog Creek ought to have a more euphonious name, the citizens decided—so it was re-named Desdemona and, during the great Eastland County oil rush, it gained world-wide renown.

The new name was bestowed in honor of the pretty daughter of the justice of the peace—and not as this story has it:

Two Easterners had invested in a well and when the drill was approaching the "sand," they journeyed to Texas to be on hand. The bit struck the "pay" and a great column of golden oil flowed over the top of the derrick.

Mr. Cohen turned to Mr. Ginsburg and said:

"Deys de money."

* * * * * * *

And speaking of cats, Brann Garner—picture show proprietor and veracious citizen of Ranger—says he has a cat that eats a plate of hot cakes every morning. Not only that, but just a few mornings ago when the hot cakes were set before Tom, he sniffed, turned up his nose and walked away. The cafe had changed cooks!

* * * * * * *

During World War I a recruit from the cattle country was A. W. O. L. from a camp near San Antonio. The military police found him standing fascinated in front of the huge electric sign of a department store, showing a cowboy roping a steer.

"I been watchin' four hours and he ain't missed yet," the rookie explained.

* * * * * * *

Derby, a town south of San Antonio, is thus accounted for:

A passenger's hat was blown off and he sprang from the train to retrieve his five-dollar derby. He had to wait so long in the lonely spot for the next train that he founded the town.

JUDGE
ROY
BEAN

Roy Bean, "the law west of the Pecos," ran the Jersey Lilly Saloon and was justice of the peace at Langtry.

One of the boys got full of whiskey and killed a Chinese laundryman. The slayer was one of the saloon's best customers.

Judge Bean searched all through his only law book—the statutes of Texas compiled twenty years before—and at last announced:

"I've looked from kiver to kiver and I can't find where it's against the law to kill a Chinaman. Case dismissed."

* * * * * *

A story based on Judge Bean's reluctance to give change is that of a lawyer who bought a glass of beer and placed a twenty-dollar gold piece on the bar. Bean was so slow about handing over any change that the barrister began to cuss.

Whereupon the old Judge said:

"I fine you $6.66 2-3 for public profanity; $6.66 2-3 for abusive language and $6.66 2-3 for public nuisance."

Then, with a grand wave, "The beer is on me."

The body of a stranger was found on the railroad track. In the pockets were a six-shooter and forty dollars.

Judge Bean fined the corpse forty dollars for carrying a concealed weapon.

* * * * * * *

Inconsistent with his previous decision was Judge Bean's ruling in another pistol-toting case.

He pointed out that the Texas law permits a man to carry a pistol if he is traveling. Then the jurist reasoned:

"If he's moving around, he's traveling and has a right to carry a gun.

"If he's standing still, he ain't carrying a pistol. Case dismissed."

* * * * * * *

The body of a man was found with a bullet-hole squarely between the eyes.

Judge Bean conducted an inquest and his verdict was:

"The deceased came to his death at the hands of an unknown party who was a d—— good pistol-shot."

* * * * * * *

Ascribed to Roy Bean (who, however, never pronounced a sentence of death), the following is a Southwestern classic:

"Carlos Morales, you have been tried by twelve good men and true; not your peers but as high above you as heaven is above hell, and they have said that you are guilty.

"In a few weeks, Spring will spread a carpet of green grass and beautiful flowers on every hill and dale; then will come hot Summer with its shimmering waves on the horizon; then Fall, with her yellow harvest moon and hills growing golden under the sinking sun; and, finally, Winter, with its howling winds and all the land clad in snow.

"But you, Carlos Morales, will not be here to see all this, for it is the order of the court that you be taken to the nearest tree and hanged by the neck until you are dead—dead—dead, you saddle-colored son-of-a-gun."

ALONG THE RIO GRANDE

Mexican canary: A burro.

* * * * * * *

A Scotchman named a burro "Maxwelton." He explained: "Maxwelton's brays are bonny."

* * * * * * *

Repeal of prohibition ruined one of the State's wheezes pertaining to the stream which divides Texas from Mexico.

The Rio Grande was described as:

"The river that is dry on one side and wet on the other."

* * * * * * *

Tequila, (usually pronounced te-kill-'em), is so heavily charged with alcohol that when the imbiber gets over a spree, he becomes intoxicated again every time he takes a drink of water.

Tequila is commonly known as "Mexican gasoline."

A newcomer in the border country heard nothing except "Mañana" (tomorrow) and "Quien sabe?" (literally, "Who knows?" but, accompanied by a shrug of the shoulders, a lift of the eyebrow, a roll of the eyes and a quick movement of the hands, it can mean everything or nothing).

One day he saw a funeral procession and, noticing a particularly intelligent-looking Mexican who—he figured—could speak English, the newcomer inquired:

"Who's dead?"

There came the inevitable "Quien sabe?"

"Fine," said the Easterner, "and I hope that other so-and-so, Mañana, dies right away."

* * * * * * *

Texas weather forecast:
Chili today and hot tamale.

* * * * * * *

"Do you understand Spanish?"
"Yes—when I'm speaking it."

* * * * * * *

It is related of a politician who later became a national figure that when he went to Austin as a member of the legislature, he brought a five-dollar bill and one shirt—and that he never changed either throughout the 90-day session.

* * * * * * *

When magnificent Palo Duro canyon in the Panhandle was discovered by a cowboy, he exclaimed, "Golly, what a gulley!"

* * * * * * *

The origin of the Palo Duro canyon: A banker dug it out trying to recover a dime he had dropped down a prairie-dog hole.

* * * * * * *

Hoover beef-steak: jack-rabbit.

FAVORITE SPORTS

In a cowboy baseball game, the batter hit a "Texas leaguer" over second base. As the center-fielder ran in to take the ball on the bounce, an old cow that had wandered into the outfield bit down on a cluster of grass—and swallowed the ball.

But the outfielder was equal to the occasion. He drove old Betsy forward and tagged the runner out with the cow as he slid into second base.

And that's no "bull!"

* * * * * * *

Amon Carter, the Fort Worth publisher, made a pep talk to the Texas Christian University football team and student body on the eve of their annual game with their greatest rivals, the Southern Methodist University Mustangs of Dallas.

"Hit 'em and hit 'em hard," he urged, and there were cheers. "Then pick 'em up, dust 'em off and knock 'em down again." (More cheers).

Dr. E. W. McDiarmid, a faculty member, who spoke next, said:

"I agree with what Mr. Carter said to you Horned Frogs—except I would say this, that if you boys do get rough with the Mustangs, be sure you do it in the proper Christian spirit."

* * * * * * *

Another favorite story of Amon Carter is one about a farmer who was kept awake by the croaking of bullfrogs in a nearby pond, so he wrote to a produce house and asked how much they would pay for a railroad tank car full of bullfrogs. They wired back that they would pay $250.

Two weeks later, he shipped seven bullfrogs and wrote a note of explanation: "Their noise fooled me."

78

Parks Camp, an oil community near Breckenridge, used to have one of the fastest semi-pro baseball teams in the State.

A most unusual event once occurred there. A ball game was in progress on a Sunday afternoon. The sky was dark with low-lying clouds. The visiting team was at bat, the score was tied and two men were out in the ninth inning.

The batter hit a liner into deep center. As the fielder raced back a bolt of lightning flashed, cutting the ball in two.

He caught one half but it looked as though the other half would fall safe.

In such an event, it would count as half a home run and would make the score 4½ to 4. It would also make two and one-half outs. The other side would insist on its right to keep batting until there were three outs. However, Parks Camp certainly would object because then the other team would wind up with three and one-half outs.

Fortunately, though, the fielder made a dive and caught the second half of the ball just before it hit the ground.

*   *   *   *   *   *   *

One of the most successful football coaches in the history of the Southwest Conference—and without a doubt the most colorful—was Francis Schmidt, who coached the Texas Christian University Horned Frogs in Fort Worth and, before that, the University of Arkansas Razorbacks in Fayetteville.

A favorite saying of his was "You can't finesse a tackle." When he left Texas to take over the job of directing the gridiron destinies of Ohio State, a reporter asked if he thought he could defeat Michigan, which seemed to have a hoodoo spell over Ohio State, Schmidt replied: "Those boys put their pants on one leg at a time, don't they?" (Ohio State won the game).

In a Southwest Conference game, the officials made a ruling against Schmidt's team. He ran out on the field and protested to the umpire, referee and head linesman but to no avail—in fact, he was ordered off the field or the game would be forfeited. He returned to the bench and a minute later the band began playing:

"Three Blind Mice."

The officials learned afterward that Schmidt had sent a note to the band director, requesting the tune!

79

When "Schmitty" was mentor of the Razorbacks, the Southern Methodist University Mustangs went to Fayetteville for a game. On the trip, an S. M. U. quarterback had lost his football shoes so the referee went to the clubhouse to borrow a pair.

"Sure," said Schmidt, ducking down into a big bin and beginning to paw among the footwear. "What size does he wear?"

"Six and a half."

The coach raised up and said, "There ain't a blankety-blank in Arkansas, male or female, with a foot that small."

* * * * * * *

Of course, these are just stories.

Schmidt, all joking aside, was a brilliant strategist, an exponent of razzle-dazzle. My favorite story about him is the one about the Baylor-T. C. U. game one season. Baylor had a trick play and Schmidt warned the Frogs against this and instructed each man what he was to do.

Sure enough, the Bears pulled the play—and scored the winning touchdown.

On Monday, coach and squad were analyzing the game.

"What happened?" Schmidt asked.

The right end replied, "I did just what you told me to do— I took care of the left halfback." And in turn each player declared that he had carried out his assignment and had taken his man out of the play.

Schmidt listened patiently and then solemnly declared:

"Boys, the play was illegal—they had 12 men on the field!"

* * * * * * *

One season, when T. C. U. played the University of California in Los Angeles, the U. C. L. A. team included four negroes—two ends and two backfield men.

A T. C. U. halfback stuck the pigskin under his arm and started around end. The left end, a negro, missed him; the right end, also colored, over-charged—missed him. Here came the left halfback, also a negro, and the T. C. U. player sidestepped him and then last of all the safety man, the fourth negro on the team, came at him but the ball-carrier stiff-armed him and flattened him out on the turf.

He was out in the open field and he looked long gone for a touchdown but from somewhere there came a tackle, a white boy, who dragged him down from behind on the 27-yard line.

The T. C. U. player jumped up, stuck out his hand and said:

"Dr. Livingstone, I presume."

80

W. J. Barnes, former West Texas prosecuting attorney, is authority for this one about a negro football game:

The battle rocked along until, with only seconds to play and the score 0-0, the team on the offensive decided to plunge the line. The ball was in midfield so it was apparently the poorest play possible from a scoring standpoint—but wait!

When the fullback hit the line, he was stopped cold and all twenty-two players piled up. There was a fumble and the ball came rolling into view. At the same time, a white man on the sideline tossed in another football.

Simultaneously, a red-sweatered player and a blue-jerseyed one arose from that wriggling mass; each grabbed a football and, heading in opposite directions, each ran fifty yards for a simultaneous touchdown!

* * * * * * *

A bunch of cowpunchers were playing baseball.

The batter knocked the ball over the right fielder's head. He ran back for the ball but a rattlesnake spied it, too, and started to swallow it.

There was a pretty situation: the batter was approaching third base and the ball was in the rattler's mouth.

But the fielder grabbed the snake by the tail, whirled the creature around his head four times and then, with a quick movement of the wrist, snapped off the snake's head and sent it—baseball and all—"plunk" into the catcher's mitt to retire the runner as he slid into home plate.

* * * * * * *

"I suppose you account for the speed of backfield men in Texas by claiming that when they were boys they ran down rabbits for the family table," an Eastern sports writer said.

"Not exactly," the Lone Star College coach replied. "They not only had to be fast enough to catch a rabbit but they had to be able to reach down while running alongside of one and feel him to see if he was plump enough to eat."

81

RATTLERS

Two cowboys were sent out one Winter to get some posts with which to repair the fence. Trees were scarce but they found a lot of queer-looking, crooked "sticks" which, on closer examination, proved to be frozen snakes—so the cowboys used them to string the wire on.

The plan worked all right till Spring came and the snakes thawed out and wriggled away, leaving three miles of fence that had to be fixed up again.

* * * * * * *

A tragedy befell Peg-leg Slim. He was bitten on his wooden leg by a rattlesnake.

The leg began to swell at once. His two comrades took turns with an axe trying to reduce the swelling but it was no use—the leg swelled faster than they could chop. So at last they had to shoot poor Slim to get him out of his suffering.

However, they had enough kindling to last all winter.

Sagebrush Sam was telling about a harrowing experience:

"The other day I was asleep under a mesquite tree when I felt a pressure and as I opened my eyes, there was a rattlesnake on my chest. He was coiled and if I made a move for my pistol or tried to jump up, he woulda struck me quick as lightnin'."

One of the others spoke up:

"What did you do?"

Sam replied:

"I saw there wasn't nothin' I could do; so I just went back to sleep."

    *   *   *   *   *   *   *

Ever have an accident?

No.

I thought a rattlesnake bit you one time.

That wasn't an accident; he did it on purpose.

    *   *   *   *   *   *   *

A rancher was irked by a rattlesnake that raided his hens' nests—so he contrived a trap.

Just outside the small hole through which the snake was accustomed to crawl into the henhouse, the ranchman placed an egg. Then he put another just inside the opening.

That night, the snake came along, swallowed the first egg, started to crawl into the hole but couldn't go all the way because of the egg he had swallowed.

Then he saw the second egg, swallowed that—and then was trapped. He could neither go forward nor backward and so fell an easy prey to the rancher the next morning.

    *   *   *   *   *   *   *

"Lotta excitement up at Horseneck today," said Cactus Pete, back in prohibition days.

"Seems that a feller captured a live rattler, brought it into town and was exhibitin' it at the drug store when it bit him.

"The druggist give him a good, big drink of likker right away.

"Another feller, and then another, was bit and, o'course, had to have some snake remedy.

"When I left town, there was a line o' men a block long in front of the rattler's pen and they was a-waitin' for him to produce more poison.

Jack Lamb, world's champion fisherman, tells this one:

A fellow was fishing one day but was having no luck. He spied a frog and, deciding that here was good bait, seized the animal just ahead of a snake.

The snake looked so reproachful that the man, deciding the critter had a kick coming, poured a drink of liquor down the snake's throat.

Then he resumed fishing, with the frog as bait, but in a little while he felt a gentle tapping against his leg. Looking down, he saw the snake—with another frog in his mouth.

* * * * * * *

A hunter reported seeing a snake so big that the reptile was in two coils!

* * * * * * *

A farmer living on the edge of town was plowing when he saw a huge snake approaching. The rattler was by far the largest he had ever seen. It must have measured twenty-four feet from the point of its nose to the tip of its tail and twenty-four feet from the tip of its tail to the point of its nose, making a total length of forty-eight feet.

The snake circled around him as the farmer stood rooted to the spot by terror. Slowly the rattler reduced the circle like a band of Comanches closing in on a stockade. When the man thought his final moment had come, he perceived that the snake was wearing a smile and the creature rubbed against his leg and purred like a cat that had lapped up cream from a contented cow.

The rattlesnake followed him home and soon became a great pet.

"Rudolph"—that was the name the farmer bestowed—used to wrap his huge form about the man's feet and keep him warm during the cold winter nights.

But one morning the farmer awakened with a start. His feet were cold. Rudolph was not there.

From the kitchen came sounds of a disturbance and the man hastened there. He took in the situation at a glance.

Rudolph had heard a burglar, had glided in and, before the intruder was aware, had wrapped himself around the man, then anchored himself with a few twists of his neck about a leg of the kitchen stove; then stuck his tail out the window and was rattling for a policeman!

84

A man fishing on the river-bank had drunk about half the contents of a jug when he happened to notice a rattler coiled near him.

The fisherman said, "Go ahead and strike; I'll never be better prepared than now."

* * * * * *

A farmer was driving a wagon to town when a rattlesnake struck at one of the mules but the team swerved sharply to one side and the fang hit the wagon-tongue. Immediately, the wagon tongue started turning black and the farmer saw that the wagon was a goner and he just did get the mules unhitched in time to save them.

* * * * * * *

Razorbacks in Texas are so thin that they sometimes crawl into the barn through the space between the logs and so their owners tie knots in their tails to keep them from falling through the cracks in the floor.

* * * * * *

During a long spell of wet weather, a farmer discovered that his hogs were pining away and about to die. He investigated and discovered that they were suffering from insomnia. As they walked around, the ball of mud on each critter's tail kept getting bigger until finally it was so heavy that it stretched their hides so tight that they couldn't close their eyes, and so could get no sleep!

* * * * * *

"I noticed in the paper this morning where a Texas man was struck by lightning while he was swearing—remarkable that it should have happened just at that time, don't you think?"

"It seems to me that it would have been more remarkable if the lightning had struck a Texan while he wasn't cussing."

HERE AND THERE

About as marvelous as Gib Morgan of the oil fields was a character known as Pecos Bill whose biography has been written by Dr. Mody Boatright of the University of Texas.

Pecos Bill arrived in Texas during a heavy storm—in fact, he slid down on a bolt of lightning.

A favorite sport with him was to spit in a rattlesnake's eye and drown it. He was so tough he used sandpaper for sheets. His lariat was made of rattlesnakes and you could hear the rattlers singing as the rope sailed through the air. He could rope a whole herd of buffalo at one toss. The most valuable thing about them was their hides and, instead of killing the animals, he just took hold of them, skinned them alive and then turned them loose to grow new hides. But one Spring he skinned 'em too early and a norther came howling along and the buffalo took pneumonia and died. And that's the way the buffalo disappeared from the Southwest, regardless of what the historians say.

First time Pecos Bill saw a train, he thought it was some new sort of varmit and he roped it and nearly wrecked the durn thing.

He used to drink his coffee boiling hot and he used a prickly pear for a napkin.

Pecos Bill was the ridingest cowboy that ever was. He bet a pair of boots he could ride a cyclone and he went up to the Kansas line, jumped on one and rode it across Oklahoma, a-curling his mustache and a-spurring that cyclone in the flanks. When it saw it couldn't throw him, it just naturally rained out from under him.

* * * * * * *

A new technique has been developed by one Texas fisherman. He cuts up chewing tobacco and throws it into the water. The fish grab the chunks and go to the bottom but they have to come to the surface to spit and that's when he hits them in the head with a club.

When the Southern Pacific Railroad was building through Texas, Pecos Bill got the contract to furnish the wood. He went to Mexico and made a deal with the natives for them to do the cutting and he would give them half of what they cut. When they got through, they had great stacks of cordwood as their share and they didn't know what to do with it, so Pecos Bill kindly took it off their hands and didn't charge them a cent.

He did the grading, too, on the Southern Pacific. He rounded up ten thousand badgers and put them to digging. He had some trouble getting them to go in a straight line and that's why the railroad has so many crooks and turns in some places.

* * * * * * *

Pecos Bill was a great ranchman. His ranch outfit was so big that he would have his cooks dam up a canyon to mix the biscuit dough in. They would dump in the flour and salt and the baking powder, and mix it with teams and fresnos.

You can still see the traces of those dough-mixing places—alkali lakes, they call them. That's the baking powder that stayed in the ground.

* * * * * * *

This story of the markmanship of David Crockett, who died in the Alamo, came from Tennessee where, it seems, he was hunting in the mountains. The "dead shot" had just aimed his rifle at a raccoon near the top of a tall tree and the 'coon said, "Don't shoot, Mr. Crockett! I'll come down."

* * * * * * *

Another Crockett story, also ante-dating his Texas days, occurred in Washington during his career as a Congressman. He was listening to a ponderous orator who declared, "Mr. Speaker, the generality of mankind in general is inclined to oppress the generality of mankind in general."

Crockett pulled him by his coat-tail and said, "Hold on, Mister; you're goin' in the same hole you just come out of."

* * * * * * *

There are many legendary tales concerning Crockett. It is recorded that he fanned himself with a hurricane, and that he shot six cords of bear in one day.

Most epic of all Davy Crockett's legendary exploits is thus set forth— (it is supposed to be Crockett himself speaking) :

One January morning, it was so cold that the forest trees were stiff and they couldn't shake, and the very daybreak was froze fast as it was tryin' to dawn. The tinder box in my cabin would no more catch fire than a raft at the bottom of the ocean.

Seein' daylight was so far behind time, I thought creation was in a fair way for freezin' fast: so, thinks, I, I must strike a little fire from my fingers, light my pipe an' travel out a few miles an' see about it.

Then I brought my knuckles together like two thunder-clouds but the sparks froze before I could begin to collect 'em, so out I walked, a-whistlin' "Fire in the Mountains."

Well, after I had walked some twenty miles up the Peak o' Day and Daybreak Hill, I found what was the trouble. The earth had actually friz fast on her axis an' couldn't turn round; the sun had got jammed between two chunks of ice under the wheels and he worked so hard to get loose that he friz fast in his own sweat.

"Creation!" thought I, "this air the tightest sort o' suspension an' it mustn't be endured; somethin' must be done or human creation is done for.

By this time it were so anteluvian and premature cold that my upper and lower teeth and tongue were all collapsed to-gether as tight as a oyster. But I took a fresh, 400-pound b'ar off my back that I'd picked up on the road, beat the animal again the ice till the hot ile began to walk out o' him at all sides. I then took an' held 'im over the earth's axis an' squeezed 'im till I'd thawed 'em loose, poured about a ton of his ile over the sun's face, give the earth's cog-wheel a few kicks back'ards till I got the sun loose and the earth give a grunt an' begun movin'.

The sun walked up beautiful, salutin' me with sich a wind o' gratitude that it made me sneeze. I lit my pipe by the blaze of his top-knot, shouldered my b'ar and walked home, intro-ducin' people to the fresh daylight with a piece of sunrise in my pocket!

*   *   *   *   *   *   *

The Trinity River is murky—so much so that the fish swim backward to keep from getting mud in their eyes.

An early settler, talking the other day, said:

"I used to live so far from the county seat that I had to grease the wagon twice on the journey; but, at that, a lot o' you fellers passed my house on your way to town."

They, no doubt, were the inhabitants who lived deep in the backwoods where the owls roosted with the chickens.

*   *   *   *   *   *   *

A boy showed up at the Dallas Fair with a hog of the razorback variety which he wanted to enter in the competition.

"He certainly wouldn't provide much pork or lard; what are you going to enter him for?" an official asked.

"Speed, by gum," said the boy. "Where I live, a hog that can't outrun a nigger won't last very long."

*   *   *   *   *   *   *

Denver Chestnutt, publisher of the Kenedy Advance, tells about a hog known as Old Blue Luther. The whole neighborhood turned out to hunt this hog down, dogs and all. The chase was successful and Old Blue Luther yielded a pint of lard, five gallons of turpentine and in his stomach was a pine knot big enough to barbecue the carcass.

*   *   *   *   *   *   *

A farmer especially interested in livestock wanted to attend the Fort Worth Fat Stock Show. He was particularly anxious to see the grand champion bull.

But when he arrived at the gate and found that it was going to cost his wife and himself 50 cents each and two oldest children half a dollar each and the other seven children 25 cents a head, he appealed to the assistant manager:

"Me an' my wife an' the children have come 200 miles to see that champion bull but we can't afford to pay $3.75 for tickets."

The official said:

"Are all those children yours?"

"Yes, sir."

"Well, all of you come right in as the guests of the management, Mister; we want that bull to see you."

*   *   *   *   *   *   *

The mosquitoes are so big along the Gulf Coast, at some points, that the inhabitants use mouse-traps to catch them.

Texas has had some remarkable dogs. For instance, the one in the Brady country whose specialty was to run a covey of quail down a prairie dog hole, put his paw over the opening till the hunter was ready, then lift the paw just long enough for one bird at a time to fly out.

* * * * * * *

Then there was one that was a great bird dog. One day he came to a "point" right on main street. There were no birds in sight and the owner called to the dog, at first quietly and then about half mad but still Tige was on a perfect point. Then the master had an idea; he asked a stranger "What is your name?" And the man answered, "My name is Bob White"—and that explained everything.

* * * * * * *

But Lometa had the prize dog of them all. The owner claimed that all he had to do was to show the dog a board and the dog would go off and find a 'possum whose hide would fit the board. This saved the man the trouble of hunting up a board to fit the hide.

One day, though, the dog disappeared and when he had been missing for three days, his master began looking for him and found him so exhausted that he had to carry him home. The only way that the man could account for the occurrence was that his wife happened to have the ironing board out on the back porch and the dog saw it and went out in the woods and wore himself out trying to find a 'possum with a hide big enough to fit the ironing board!

* * * * * * *

In early days, there was a ferry across a river in East Texas. A man said:

"I want to cross but I ain't got a nickel for the fare."

The ferryman replied:

"A fellow who ain't got five cents is just as well off on one side of the river as the other."

* * * * * * *

A checker game was in progress in the cross roads store, with the merchant and a friend as opponents. A customer entered but the storekeeper whispered to his adversary:

"Don't say anything; maybe he'll go away."

An inhabitant of deep East Texas was complaining that as he was driving along in his flivver, the driver of a big car had almost forced him into the ditch and had cussed him out as a "snuff-dipping so-and-so."

"Why didn't you cuss him back?" a friend inquired.

"I couldn't," the other said. "My mouth was full o' snuff at the time."

* * * * * * *

A county agent pointed out that his hog, by scientific feeding, in six months had grown to be as big as a farmer's hog had in a year. But the farmer was unimpressed and asked:

"What the he—— is time to a hog?"

* * * * * * *

A backwoodsman who had never seen a telephone was in town one day and asked the storekeeper what he was talking into a little box for. The merchant explained what the new-fangled thing was and to prove to the "doubting Thomas" that it really worked, phoned the home where the farmer's wife was visiting.

"Put Mrs. Corntassel on the line," he said and handed the receiver to the farmer.

Just then a bolt of lightning hit the line and knocked the old fellow sprawling.

"That's her all right," he said.

* * * * * * *

A sign on a tree in Eastland read:
"Don't hitch your horses here—Church Property."
Someone pencilled beneath:
"And yet Jesus Christ was born in a livery stable."

* * * * * * *

Back in the days when the Ku Klux Klan had many thousands of members in Texas, an outspoken foe of the hooded order heard that there was to be a parade. Curious to see the procession, he hastened to town but saw no fiery cross, no ghostly figures and no crowd. He decided he must have been too late, and, seeing a negro, he asked:

"George, have you seen anything of a bunch of blankety-blanks in bed-sheets?"

The darkey replied:

"Naw, suh, boss, but I seed about nine hundred white-robed gem'men go by jest now."

Along about 1924 (we have it from an indisputable source) a big, rugged fellow drove into Eastland in a buggy drawn by a tiger and was using a live rattlesnake for a whip.

Entering a drug store, he called for a drink of carbolic acid and asked for sulphuric acid as a chaser.

"Gee," said an awestruck observer, "you're tough."

"Naw," the other answered modestly, "I'm just a jelly-bean from Mer Rouge, La., that the Ku Klux drove out."

* * * * * * *

One of the best known newspaper correspondents at the State Capitol is Byron Utecht of the Forth Worth Star-Telegram.

He was introduced one day to a stranger who repeated:

"Utecht! What an odd name! Where were you born? How long have you been in this country? You speak English very well."

Utecht, an American for generations back, answered the questions politely but afterward he asked someone:

"Who was that bird that was making fun of my name?"

"Why, that was Gutzon Borglum" was the reply.

* * * * * * *

Gene Howe, the "tactless Texan" of the Amarillo News and Globe, asks:

"Did I ever tell you about that article I wrote for the Saturday Evening Post? Of course, they didn't buy it but I did write it for them."

(Later he broke into the columns of that magazine).

* * * * * * *

When the Fort Worth Star-Telegram merged with the Fort Worth Record, one sub-editor who lost out said:

"When I took this place 14 years ago, I knew this job would only be temporary."

* * * * * * *

Over in the East Texas "piney woods" region, where hunting is one of the chief purposes of living, a boy climbed up in a tree to dislodge a 'possum but a limb gave way and the youth fell to the ground, sustaining a broken back.

His companions bore him home where his father received the tidings philosophically.

"It coulda been worse," he observed. "George mighta fell on one o'the dawgs."

Brother Jones, member of a backwoods church, was so argumentative and headstrong that he was always causing trouble. One night at prayer-meeting, a member said:

"Brethren and sisters, I wish Brother Jones was in h——."

The minister interrupted:

"I'm shocked at such a wish."

"Well," the member explained, "I figger if Brother Jones was in h——, he'd have it busted up in six months."

* * * * * * *

Wonderful restorations to health have been rightly credited to the pure, dry air of Southwest Texas.

However, when the natives jest about the climate, they sometimes say that there was only one cure from the "white plague" and that was a woman who came into the region in the last stages. Accompanying her were her husband, two small children and a maid-of-all-work, Mary, an attractive girl.

The dying woman called her husband to her bedside and said:

"John, I have only a few hours to live. I want you to promise me that when I'm gone, you and Mary will marry—you need someone to look after the children."

The husband said, "Yes, darling; Mary and I have already talked it over."

"Is that so?" the wife exclaimed. "Well, I'll show you," and she proceeded to recover at once just for spite.

* * * * * * *

When Texans and Californians meet, then comes the tug of war.

On one such occasion, the Californian had a Roland for each Oliver.

At last the Texan pointed to a noble Parker County watermelon.

"You can't beat that in California," he boasted.

"What a puny-looking watermelon," said the other, contemptuously.

"Watermelon, nothing!" snorted the Texan. "Man, get away from that grape!"

* * * * * * *

Definition of an editor in West Texas:

"A printer with his brains knocked out."

(A printer gave the definition).

Over in deep East Texas, a rural church had a member whose faith and works were of the purest ray serene. He had one flaw, however—he would exaggerate.

At last the congregation decided to have a committee wait on him. The spokesman said:

"Brother Smithers, you are a fine man and a great church member but you have a fault and you must do something about it."

To which he answered:

"Brethren, I know what you are talking about and I want to tell you that I have shed barrels and barrels of tears about it."

* * * * * * *

Back to Texas has floated the strange tale of a hotel in Washington known as "The States."

The rooms are not numbered; they are named for the different commonwealths.

A visitor relates that he was shown several rooms. "Texas," named for his own State, was big enough to drill a regiment in. But it was already taken. In fact, all the rooms were rented except Rhode Island so he had to take that one.

"It was so small that the furniture was painted on the wall," he said. "They gave me a crutch to keep me in bed.

"Why the room was so little that I had to go out in the hall to change my mind and I had to teach my dog to wag his tail up and down—there wasn't space sideways."

* * * * * * *

A Texan was joshing a citizen of Arkansas. The latter—weary of endless jests concerning the Slow Train and the Arkansaw Traveler—said:

"Well, there's one thing that can be said about my State; we don't have any insane asylums."

The suprised Texan exclaimed:

"What, no asylums! Surely, some of the people become insane."

"Oh, yes."

"Then what do you do with them?" the Texan asked.

"Oh, we ship 'em to Texas and you elect 'em to the legislature."

Here is Hick Halcomb's explanation of the unusual spelling of his name:

The name was spelled *Holcomb* until Uncle Jeb, over in Witherspoon County, was found with a rope in his hand. The other end of the rope, in some unaccountable way, had become fastened about the neck of a cow belonging to someone else.

"Well, Jeb, we got you this time," the sheriff said.

Uncle Jeb was slow-moving but fast-thinking and he asked "Where's your papers, Sheriff?"

The officer fumbled around in his coat pocket and triumphantly brought out a crumpled-up warrant. Uncle Jeb took it calmly and, very nonchalantly, reached up into the breast-pocket of his overalls (they were white overalls, having bleached out) and drew forth his Sears-Roebuck glasses (twenty-five cents, one lens cracked) and adjusted them with great care on the geometric center of his bulbous nose. About the only thing that Uncle Jeb could read was his name and he looked at that now —scribbled on the outside of the warrant. After considerable deliberation, he said:

"Sheriff, you've got the wrong man. I spell my name H-A-L not H-O-L."

The puzzled sheriff took the warrant back and retreated.

And we've had to spell the name that way ever since to keep Uncle Jeb out of the pen.

* * * * * * *

There is a little sequel to Hick's narrative. He related:

I told this story some time ago to a man who lived in Witherspoon County. He claimed he didn't know Uncle Jeb and had never heard of him but that he was going to look him up when he got back home. I think he was inferring that I was telling a big lie.

Anyway, I saw him a few weeks ago and he said by the eternals he'd hunted all over Witherspoon County and he couldn't find no Jeb Halcomb and he said it jest as if to say that I was a d—— liar. But, like my illustrious uncle, I was too quick for him. I asked:

"How long did you look for him?"

"About a year."

'Well, the *Revenuers* been lookin' for him for *fourteen* years and they ain't found him."

In a one-room schoolhouse over near the Louisiana line, the new instructor was trying to impress her teaching ability upon a trustee who was visiting the school.

"Johnny," she asked one little fellow, "who killed Abel?"

"I don't know, ma'am," he answered, "but it wasn't me; I ain't lived here but two weeks."

The trustee leaned over and said to the teacher:

"Question him close; he acts mighty suspicious to me."

* * * * * * *

A West Texas editor, hard-pressed for something with which to fill his columns one week, set up the Ten Commandments and ran them without comment.

Two days later he received a letter:

"Cancel my subscription; you're getting too d—— personal."

* * * * * * *

Back in the days when the collector of these stories was working on the staff of the Fort Worth Star-Telegram, the state editor heard one morning that there had been a fire in a little town the night before and so he called the local correspondent. The latter had just gotten in from a trip and had heard of no fire but promised to investigate and phone back, which he did in a few minutes:

"It wasn't in town; it was just a farmhouse and it wasn't much of a fire."

"Thanks for phoning"—and the editor was about to hang up.

"By the way, one of the children was burned to death."

"What!"

"And another one of the children is not expected to live. Also the father and mother were burned about the hands and face in trying to rescue the children. The farmer threw the little baby out the window and it didn't get a scratch. Also, he had sold his peanut crop the day before and the money was in the house and it was burned up."

"I see—it wasn't much of a fire; one dead, one dying, two others burned, baby has miraculous escape and the earnings of an entire year destroyed."

"That's right—and, by the way, DeLeon plays football here Friday afternoon and you tell Boyce House we want a darn good write-up."

"The gwinter is jes' about the most remarkable animal that Texas ever had," drawled Cactus Joe. "I say 'had' because as fur as I know they're extinct."

In reply to the tenderfoot's question, the old cowhand continued:

"A gwinter was something like a mountain goat and a buffalo but the most remarkable thing about him was his legs—the two on one side were longer than the two on the other side.

"This met with the gwinter's approval because he would graze while walking around a mountain and so his body was kept on even keel, as he walked with his longer legs on the downside of the mountain."

Alkali Ike broke in with:

"And, say, young feller, if one ever comes chargin' at you— there may still be a few away back in them mountains, don't run because he's too fast fer you. Jes' stand yore ground till he's about four paces from you and then jump quickly to one side, preferably downward.

"Why? Because the gwinter has to run clear around the mountain to get a step lower, by which time you can be far from there."

Cactus Joe took up the lesson in natural history:

"Funny thing is that not all the gwinters has their long legs on the same side of the body. Naw, there's right gwinters and left gwinters. The right gwinters go around a mountain in one direction and the left gwinters go around it in the other direction.

"And sometimes they meet and o' course neither can pass the other and that makes 'em mad and they fights and usually kills each other.

"And that's why they's extinct, or soon will be," Cactus Joe concluded, sadly.

*   *   *   *   *   *   *

Heard in a hotel lobby at Cotulla:

One of the problems in covered wagon days on the treeless plains was that of fuel. It was solved by the use of cow-chips. Some pioneer poet has immortalized the gold rush era:

> "We crossed the plains in other days;
> We bathed in Salt Lake's brine;
> We burnt that stuff you're peddling now—
> In Eighteen Forty-Nine."

The other day a bunch of the fellows were sitting on the side-walk out in front of the general store, spitting in the street. The Old Timer was present, sitting in the street and spitting on the sidewalk, just to be different. He spoke up:

"Just heard from my brother out in the oil field. His company finished a well that is producing 6,000 barrels of castor oil a day."

There was a little murmur of disbelief which he ignored:

"I found a castor oil spring myself one time. I was the sole survivor of a wreck in the South Seas and landed on a desert island. Didn't have no food nor water, so as soon as I landed on this place I went hunting and, the first thing I found was a castor oil spring.

"That was just one of the remarkable things I found on this here island. About two hundred yards from the spring was a jelly-roll mine. There was raspberry, apple, strawberry and cinnamon rolls in this mine and I lived on them for months while I made further trips into the interior.

"The next discovery I made was a geyser that spouted 3.2 beer every twenty-two minutes. I timed it by a sundial I made so the time might not have been exactly twenty-two minutes, as my sundial was not so very accurate; it would lose ten or fifteen minutes a day, generally.

"On the north of this here island, I found a hammer tree and plucked me a good, stout claw-hammer. With this and a sawfish and a square from a squarehead shark, I was able to build me a sixteen-room cabin with two baths and servants' quarters.

"All this time I didn't have no clothes and was all the time embarrassed by my own presence. But shortly after I finished my house, I found a thrifty bloomer-bush in full fruit and picked me a pair of pants. This plant only bloomed once in seven years but that didn't bother me much as I am a married man and so one new pair of pants every seven years was just about right.

"I stayed there twenty-seven years—but my most important discovery there was a vibrating cow that gave vanilla milk-shakes."

As an out-of-State motorist was driving slowly through the most barren portion of the western part of the State, he saw a man sitting in the doorway of a one-room shack. The settler said, "I ain't as pore as you think; I don't own this place."

* * * * * * *

Out in that same general region, an Eastern soldier in training in World War II remarked to a buddy, as he gazed at the vast stretch of sand and cactus, "And, just think, we're fighting a war to save this!"

* * * * * * *

When things were looking darkest for the Allied Cause, just after the fall of France, a West Texas cowboy said, "Hitler may land a big army and take Houston and he may take Waco and Abilene too, but when he gets out here to Shallowater, he's going to have the d——dest fight he ever saw!"

* * * * * * *

A new arrival in heaven was looking around the Celestial City when, to his amazement, he noticed two men chained to a post. He turned to the angel who was acting as his guide, for an explanation. The angel said, "Those are a couple of durn fools from Texas; if we don't keep them chained up, they'll go back."

* * * * * * *

A one-time governor of Texas, whose learning was limited, was visiting a ranch and decided he'd like to do some hunting, so he phoned his office and asked his secretary to send his gun. The secretary said, "The connection is poor; I can't catch that word; please spell it." The governor replied:

"G as in Jesus; U as in onion; N as in pneumonia—GUN, you durn fool!"

* * * * * * *

A candidate for county judge in a Central Texas county was called one night over long distance by his manager in the southwest corner of the county, who said:

"Bill, they're tellin' it down here that you ain't drawed a sober breath since May 10 when you announced."

The candidate replied:

"You didn't wake me up in the middle of the night to tell me that, did you? I can't pay any attention to such a statement as that; I'm too busy fighting false rumors!"

99

"You talk about hard times but I see that you are able to have a hired hand," a visitor said to a North Texas farmer. "How much do you pay him?"

The farmer answered, "I agree to pay him thirty dollars a month and his board but the farm don't make enough to pay him anything."

"Well, how do you manage?"

"Oh, we keep on till I owe him as much as the farm is worth and then I give him the farm and I work for him. The place has changed hands that way four times."

* * * * * * *

Back in the days when Eastland County was known as "the egg-basket of Texas," one poultryman conceived the idea of mixing sawdust with the feed. He tried the experiment with one hen but quit when she laid a knot-hole!

* * * * * * *

Two Texas darkies were talking soon after Pearl Harbor. One said:

"Dem Japs an' Germans is liable to bomb Houston."

"You is right," his companion agreed.

"An' dey might bomb Dallas."

"Dat's so."

"An' dey could bomb Fort Worth."

"Nah, suh, not Fort Worth! Mr. Amon Carter wouldn't stand for dat!

* * * * * * *

A New England general was inspecting one of the numerous World War II army camps in Texas and was being shown around by a Texas general, who kept telling about Sam Houston, Crockett, Bowie and other heroes of the Lone Star State. At last the visitor interrupted:

"That's all very well but you don't have a Paul Revere."

"Paul Revere?" the Texan repeated the name as though it was vaguely familiar. Then his face brightened:

"Oh, you mean that fellow that rode around all night yelling for help? No, we don't have anybody like that."

* * * * * * *

Sign in Los Angeles:
"Buy bonds and help Texas win the war."

USE THESE PAGES TO ADD OTHER JOKES

www.ingramcontent.com/pod-product-compliance
Lightning Source LLC
Chambersburg PA
CBHW020154180626
46810CB00004B/1883